Enrich Book

Grade K

PROVIDES Daily Enrichment Activities

HOUGHTON MIFFLIN HARCOURT

Printed in the U.S.A.

ISBN 978-0-547-58817-9

2 3 4 5 6 7 8 9 10 0982 20 19 18 17 16 15 14 13 12 11

4500319268 B C D E F G

Contents

CRITICAL AREA 1: Number and Operations

Chapter 1: Represent, Count, and Write Numbers 0 to 5

Chapter 2: Compare Numbers to 5

Chapter 3: Represent, Count, and Write Numbers 6 to 9

Chapter 4: Represent and Compare Numbers to 10

Chapter 5: Addition

Chapter 6: Subtraction

Chapter 7: Represent, Count, and Write 11 to 19

CRITICAL AREA 2: Geometry and Positions

Chapter 8: Represent, Count, and Write 20 and Beyond

Chapter 9: Identify and Describe Two-Dimensional Shapes

Chapter 10: Identify and Describe Three-Dimensional Shapes

CRITICAL AREA 3: Measurement and Data

Chapter 11: Measurement

Chapter 12: Classify and Sort Data

Name ____________________

COMMON CORE STANDARD CC.K.CC.4a
Count to tell the number of objects.

Apple Picking

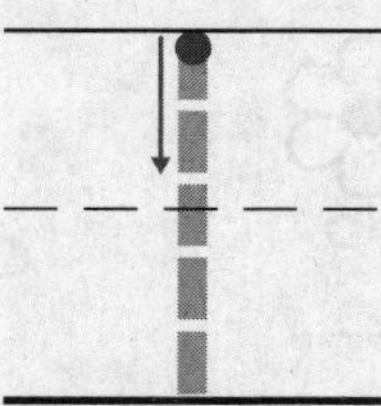

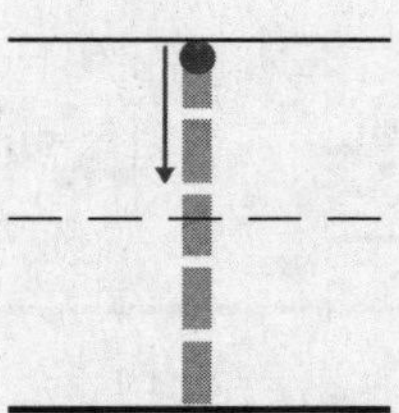

DIRECTIONS 1–4. Trace the number. Draw a line from the number to the matching number of apples. Use green to color the apples that show the number 1. Use red to color the apples that show the number 2.

Name ____________________

COMMON CORE STANDARD CC.K.CC.3
Know number names and the count sequence.

Hide and Seek

1

2

3

4

5

6

DIRECTIONS **1–6.** Find the animals. Count and write how many. Use red crayon to circle the sets of one animal. Use blue crayon to circle the sets of two animals.

Name ______________________

COMMON CORE STANDARD CC.K.CC.4a
Count to tell the number of objects.

Dot the Ladybug

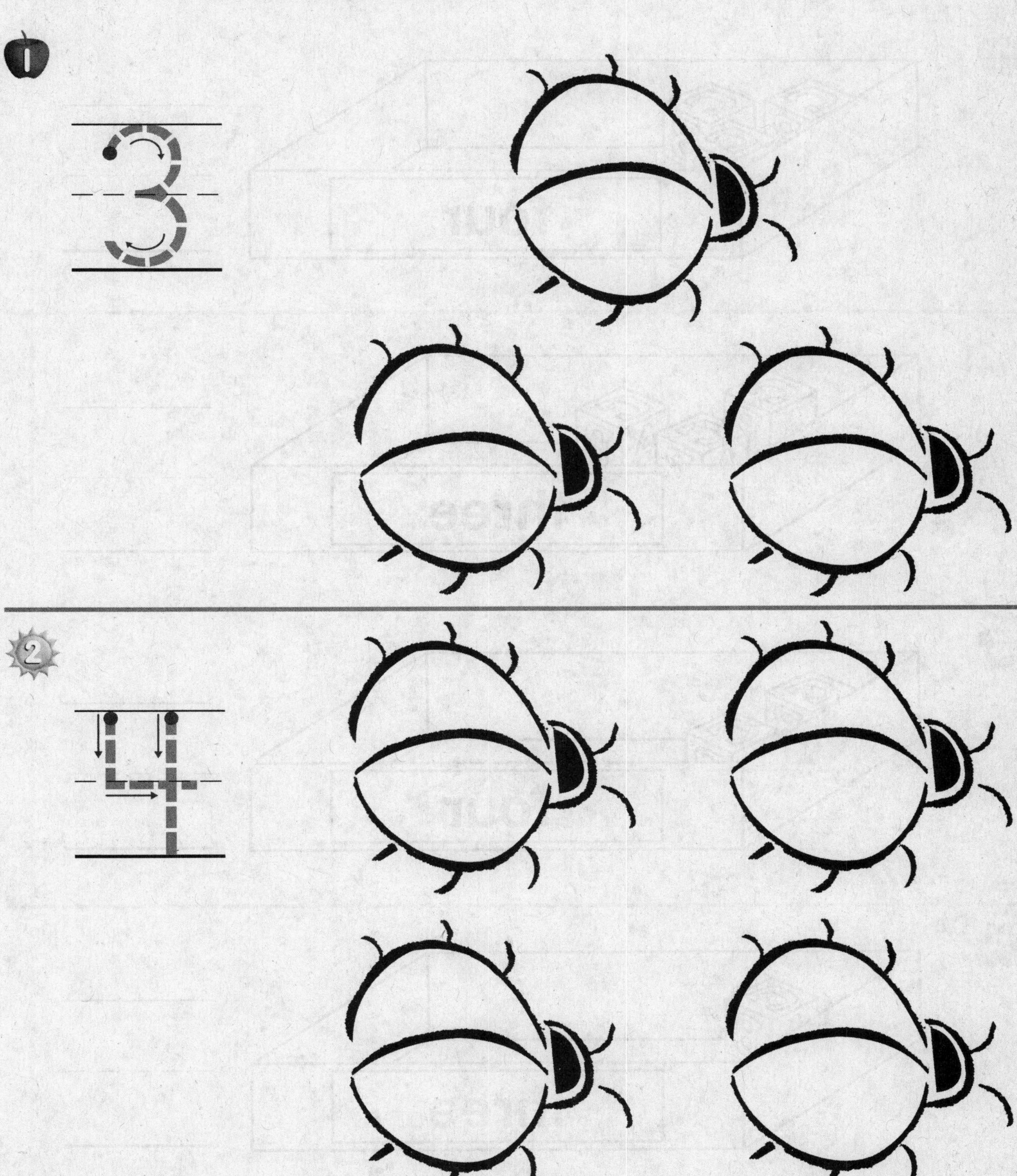

DIRECTIONS 1–2. Trace the number. Draw dots on the wings of each ladybug to show ways to place that number of dots.

Name ______________________

Clean Up Your Blocks!

COMMON CORE STANDARD CC.K.CC.3
Know number names and the count sequence.

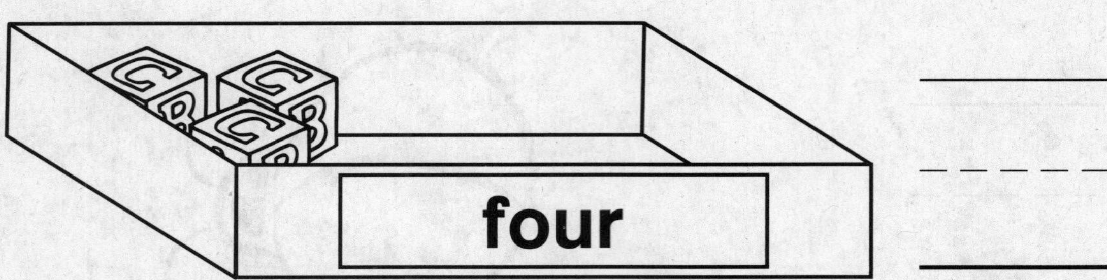

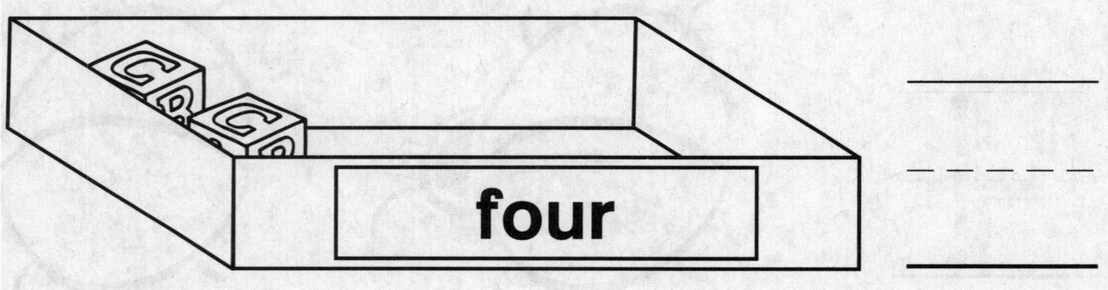

DIRECTIONS 1–4. Read the number word. Draw more blocks if needed to match the number word. Write the number.

Name ______________________

COMMON CORE STANDARD CC.K.CC.4a
Count to tell the number of objects.

Picnic Counting

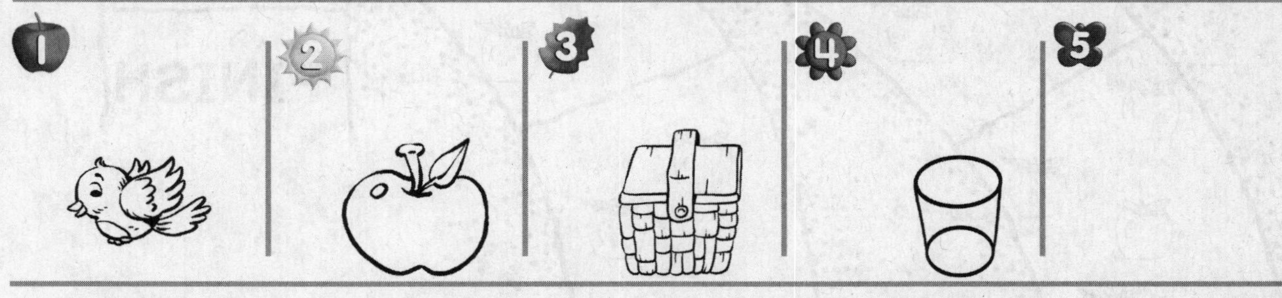

DIRECTIONS 1–4. Find each object in the picture. Count how many. Write how many more you need to have 5. **5.** Choose one more object from the picture. Draw the object. Then count and write how many more you need to have 5.

Name ______________________________

COMMON CORE STANDARD CC.K.CC.4b
Count to tell the number of objects.

Count the Way

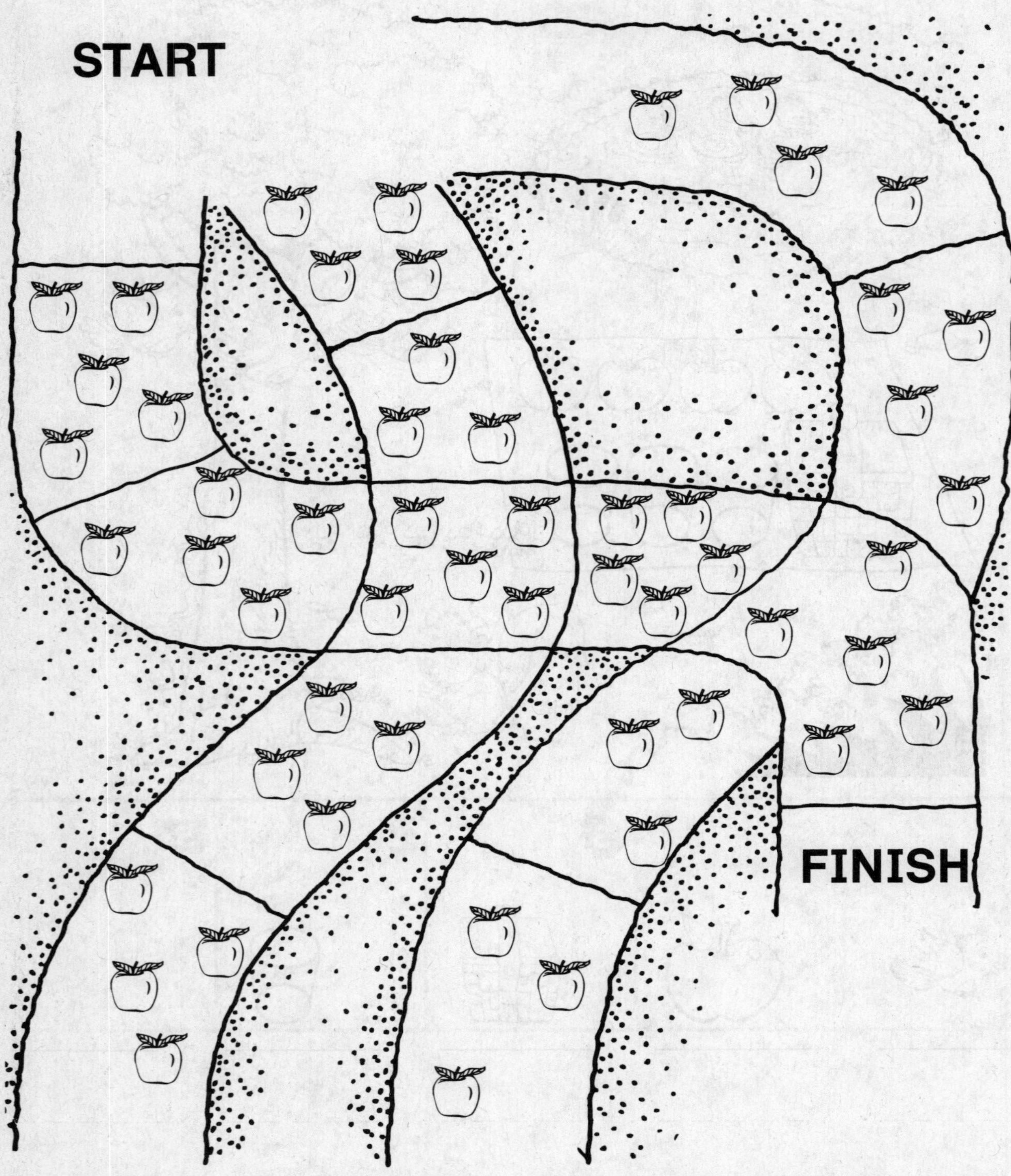

DIRECTIONS **1.** Use red to color the sets of 5 apples. Begin at START and trace a path through the sets of 5 until you reach FINISH. **2.** Draw more apples in the other sets to make 5.

Name ______________________

Flower Power

COMMON CORE STANDARD CC.K.OA.3
Understand addition as putting together and adding to, and understand subtraction as taking apart and taking from.

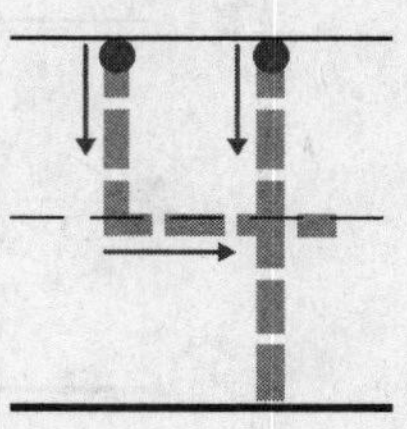

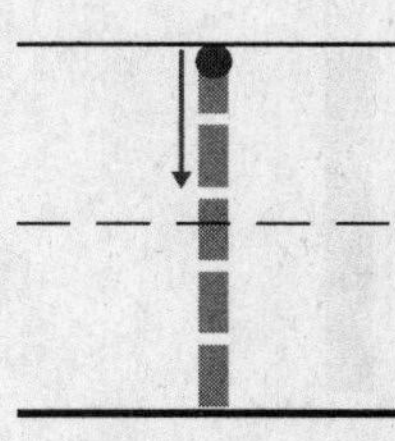

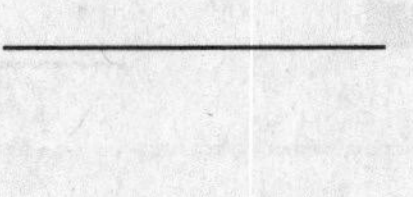

DIRECTIONS **1.** Trace the number to show how many petals. Draw one more petal to make 5 petals. Trace the number to show how many petals you drew. **2–3.** Write the number to show how many petals. Draw more petals to make 5 petals. Write the number to show how many petals you drew.

Name ____________________

Number Order

COMMON CORE STANDARD CC.K.CC.4c
Count to tell the number of objects.

1. 1 2 ___ 4 5

2. 1 ___ 3 4 ___

3. ___ 2 ___ ___ 5

4. 5 ___ ___ ___ 1

DIRECTIONS **1–3.** Write the numbers in order. **4.** Write the numbers in order from 5 to 1.

Name ______________________

Lesson 1.9
Enrich

How Many Do I Have?

COMMON CORE STANDARD CC.K.CC.3
Know number names and the count sequence.

1

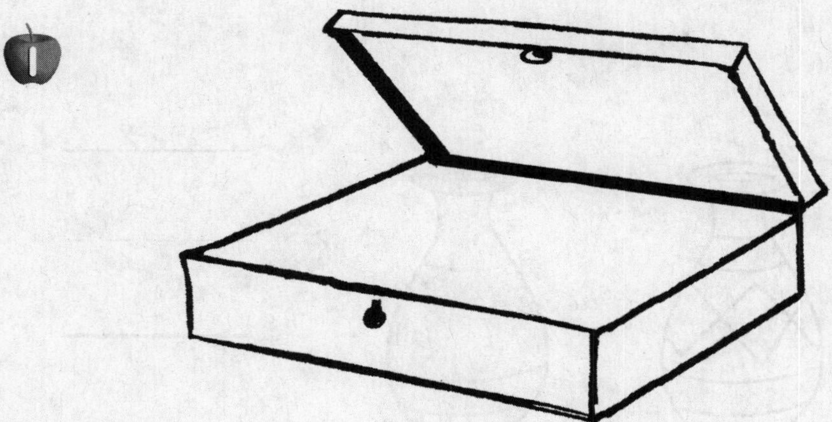

2

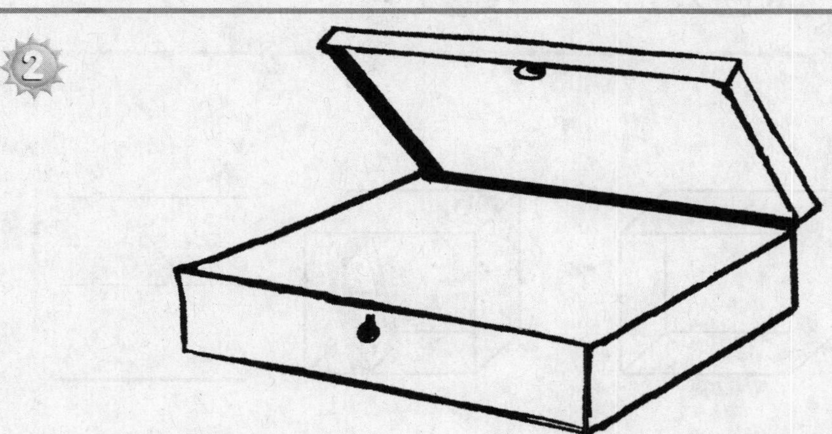

3

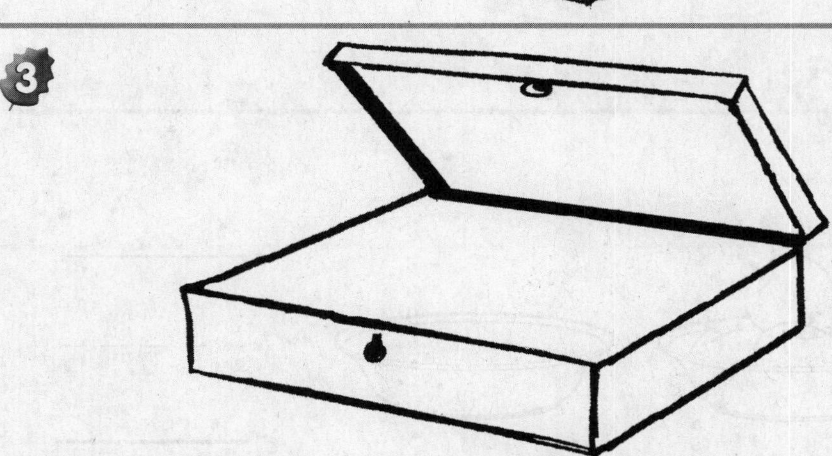

DIRECTIONS Use counters to model the problems. **1.** Ed has 2 crayons. Ann gives him 2 more crayons. Ed gives 4 crayons to Jill. How many crayons does Ed have now? Write how many. **2.** Al has 5 pencils. Kate has 3 pencils fewer than Al. Kate gives 1 pencil to Joe. How many pencils does Kate have? Write how many. **3.** Pete has 3 markers. Lee has 2 more markers than Pete. Lee gives 5 markers to Tami. How many markers does Lee have? Write how many.

Name ________________________

COMMON CORE STANDARD CC.K.CC.3
Know number names and the count sequence.

Who Am I?

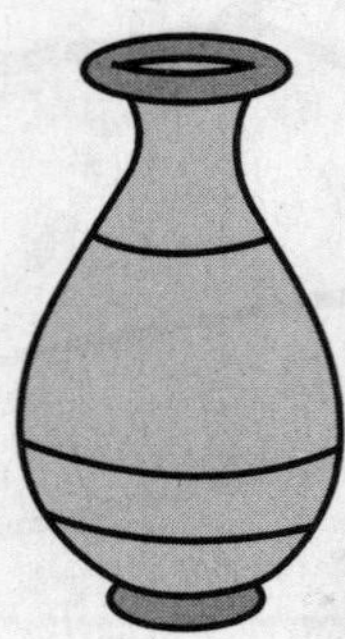

______

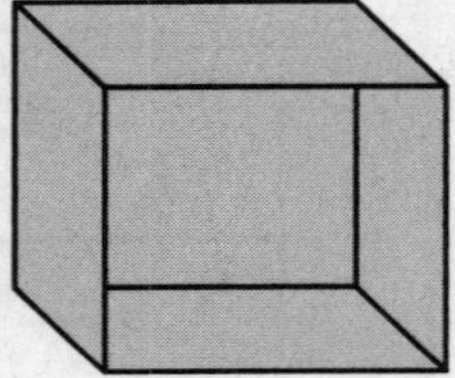
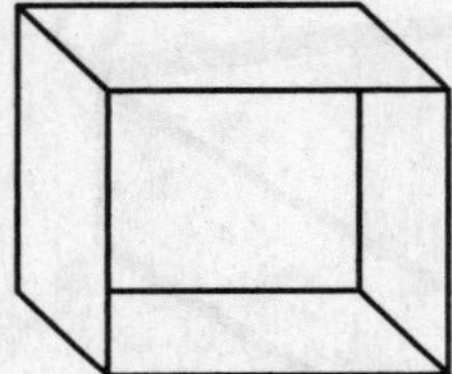

______

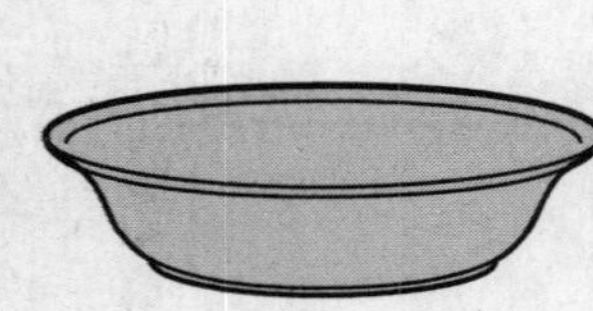

______

DIRECTIONS Listen to the clues. Circle the correct object. Write how many are in it. **1.** I am white. I have 1 fewer than 1 flower. **2.** I am gray. I have 1 more than 0 books. **3.** I am white. I have 2 fewer than 2 apples.

Name ______________________

Matching Gardens

COMMON CORE STANDARD CC.K.CC.6
Compare numbers.

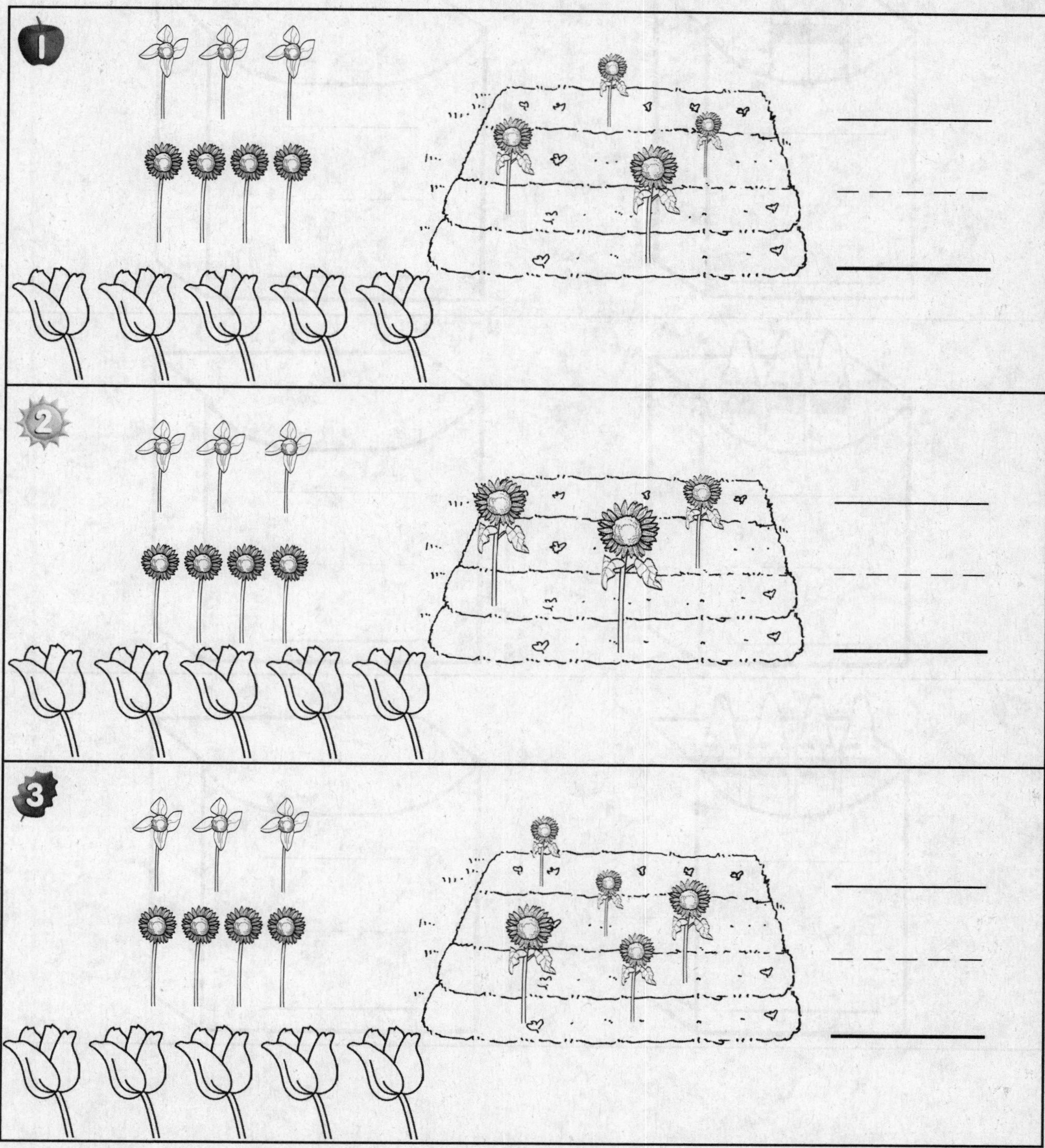

DIRECTIONS **1–3.** Count the flowers in each row. Circle the row with the same number of flowers that are planted in the garden. Write the number. Draw more flowers or mark an X on some flowers in the other rows to make them match.

Name ______________________________

COMMON CORE STANDARD CC.K.CC.6
Compare numbers.

A Greater Number

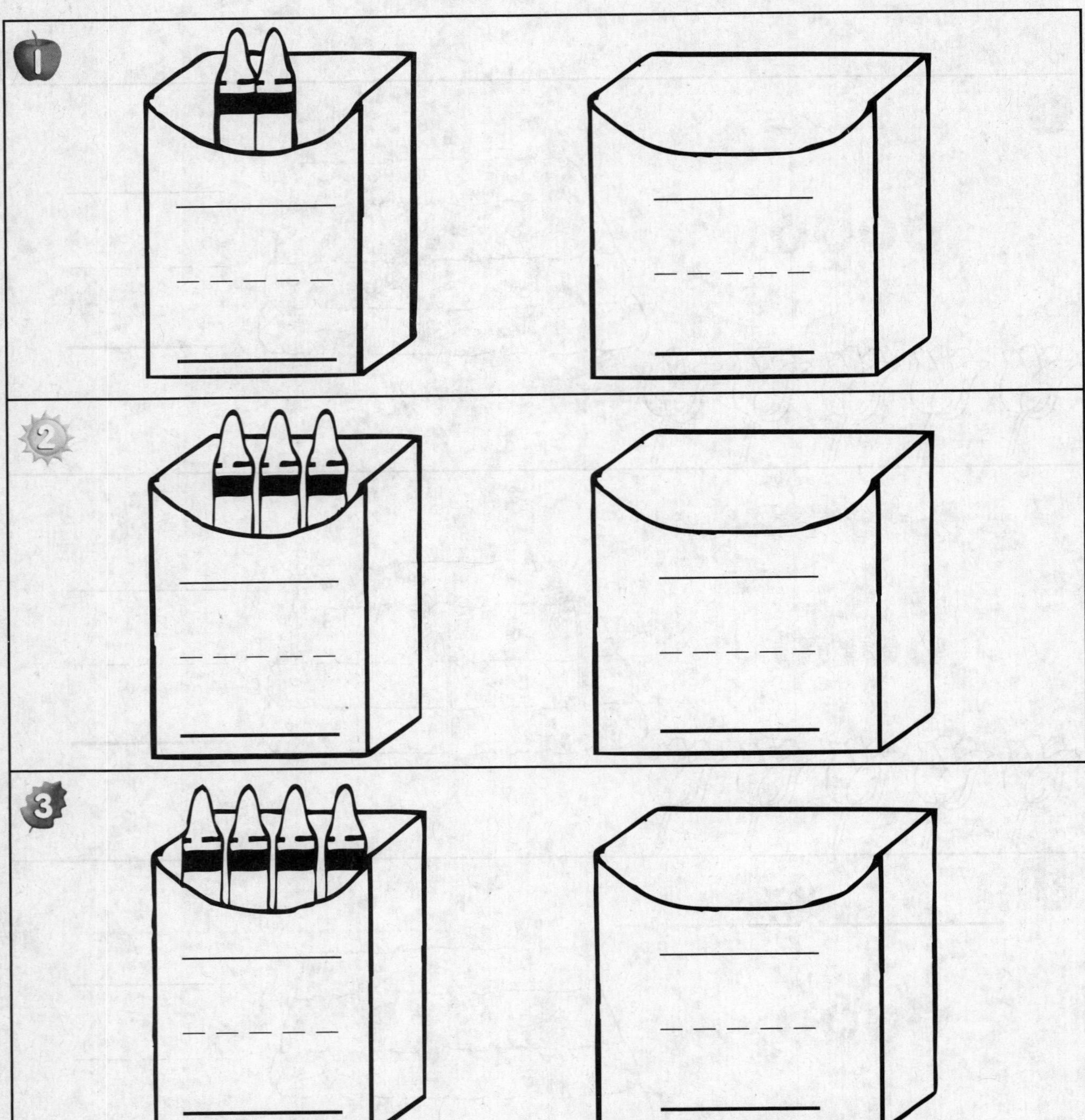

DIRECTIONS 1–3. Count the crayons in the first box. Write the number. Write a greater number on the second box. Draw the crayons.

Name ______________________

COMMON CORE STANDARD CC.K.CC.6
Compare numbers.

Play with Dot Cards

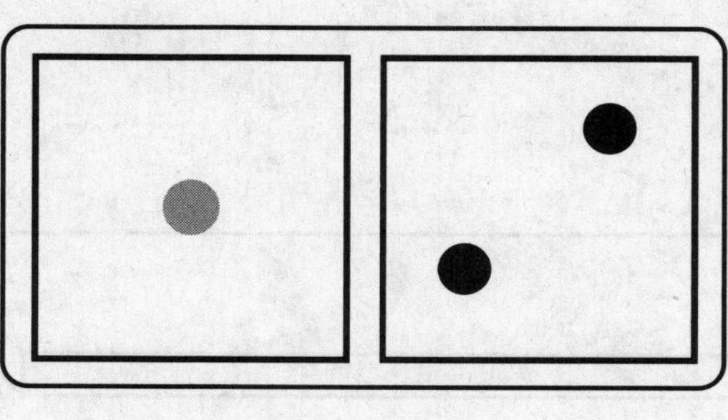

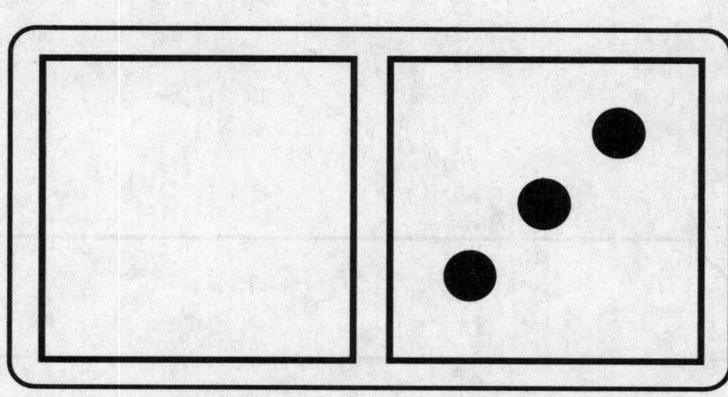

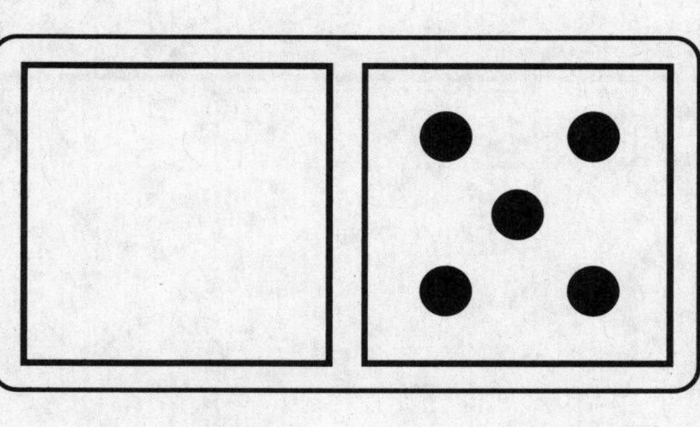

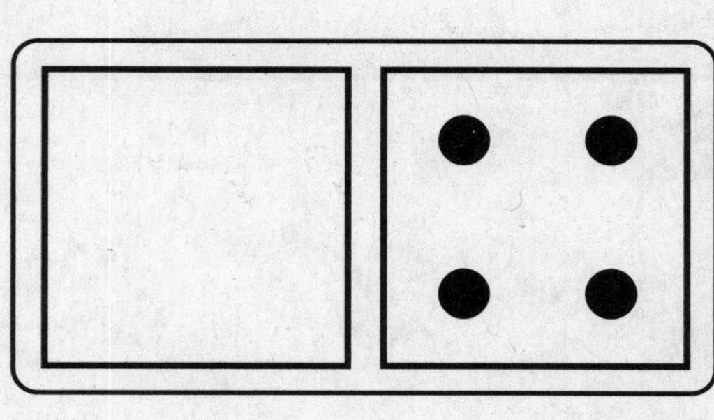

DIRECTIONS **1–4.** Count the dots on the card on the right. Write the number. Then write a number that is less. Draw dots for that number on the card on the left.

Name ______________________________

COMMON CORE STANDARD CC.K.CC.6
Compare numbers.

Time for a Picnic

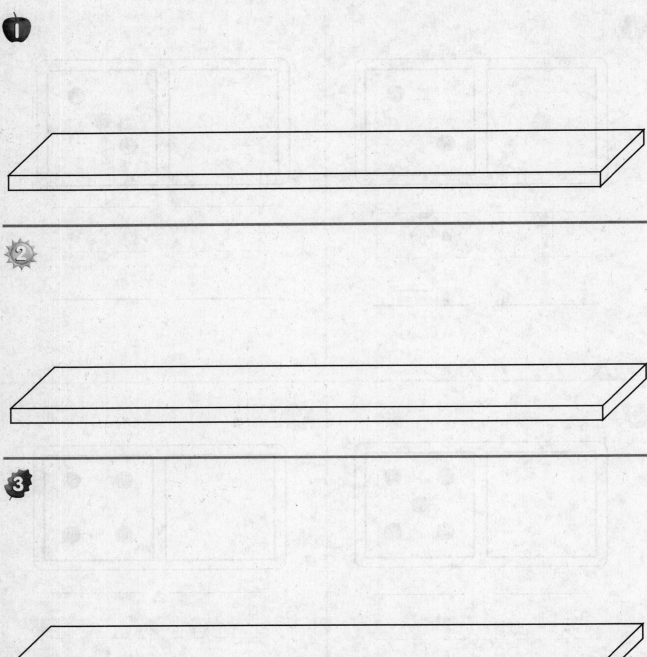

DIRECTIONS Anita goes to the supply closet to get items for a picnic. Draw the supplies she sees. **1.** The number of cups is greater than 2 and less than 4. **2.** The number of plates is greater than 3 and less than 5. **3.** A number of napkins that is greater than 1 and less than 5.

Name ______________________

Lesson 2.5
Enrich

COMMON CORE STANDARD CC.K.CC.6
Compare numbers.

Sticker Time

1

2

3

DIRECTIONS 1–3. Count and tell how many stickers there are. Write the number. Draw a set that has a number of stickers that is greater. Draw a set that has a number of stickers that is less.

Name ______________________

Crafty 6

COMMON CORE STANDARD CC.K.CC.5
Count to tell the number of objects.

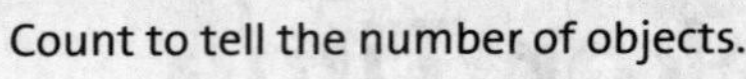

1

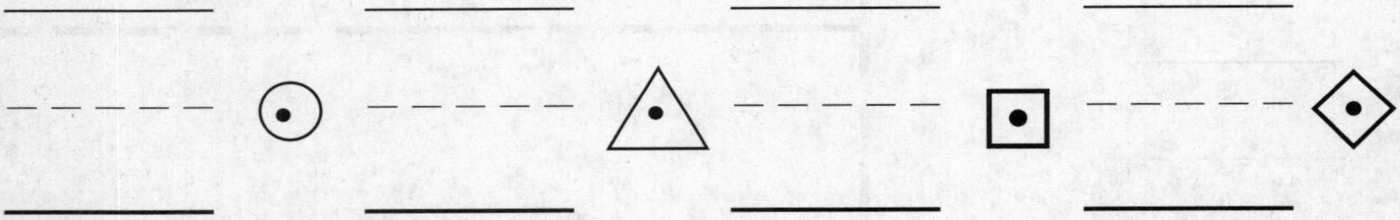

2

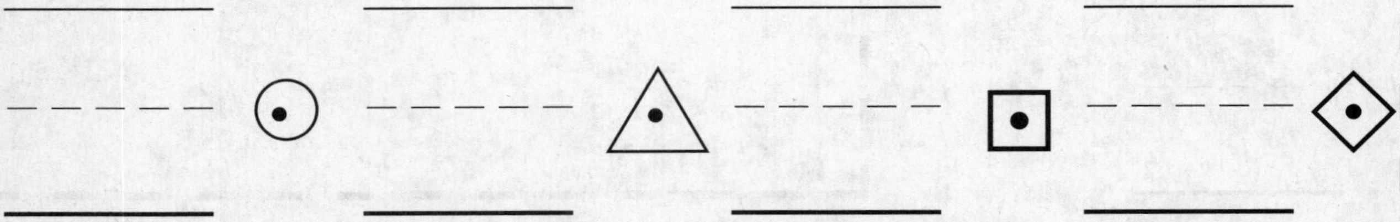

DIRECTIONS 1–2. Use the beads in the jars to draw a bead necklace with six beads. Count the beads as you draw them. Write how many of each bead.

Name ________________________________

COMMON CORE STANDARD CC.K.CC.3
Know number names and the count sequence.

Find the Path

two	three	five	three
one	two	six	one
four	three	four	two
six	one	five	six

DIRECTIONS Make a path of number words in order from one to six. Go only one space across, up, or down each time.

Name ______________________________

Swim, Sun, and 7

COMMON CORE STANDARD CC.K.CC.5
Count to tell the number of objects.

1

2

3

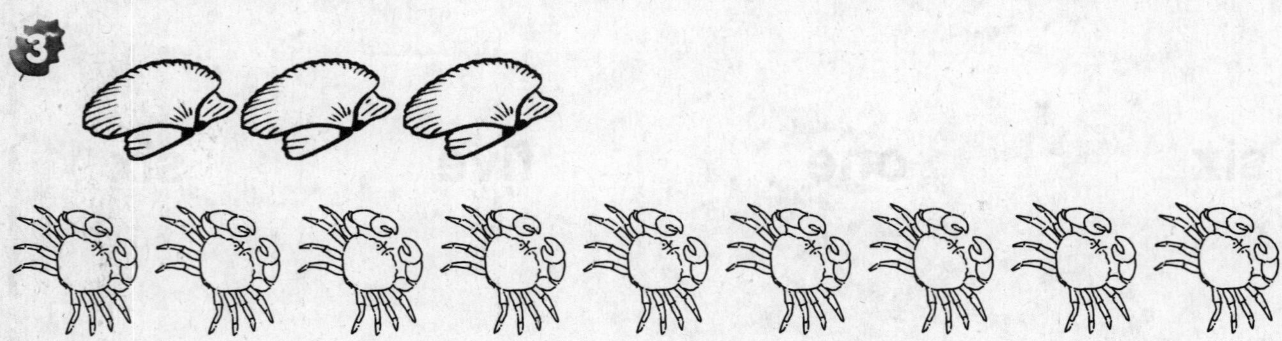

DIRECTIONS **1–3.** Count how many are in each group. Draw more or mark an X on some if needed to make 7.

Name ________________________________

Lesson 3.4
Enrich

COMMON CORE STANDARD CC.K.CC.3
Know number names and the count sequence.

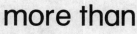

Number Art

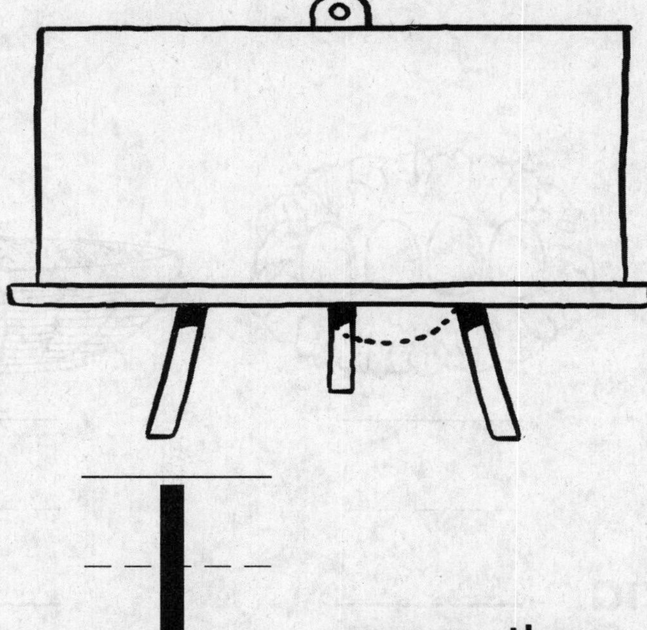

Seven is **1** more than ______.

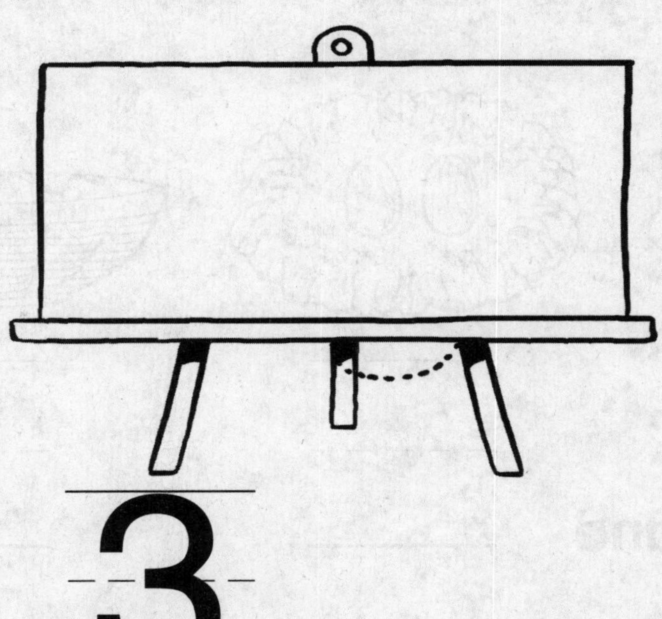

Four is **3** less than ______.

DIRECTIONS **1.** Seven is 1 more than what number? Write the number. Draw a picture to show 7. **2.** Four is 3 less than what number? Write the number. Draw a picture to show four.

Name ____________________

COMMON CORE STANDARD CC.K.CC.5
Count to tell the number of objects.

Counting Eggs

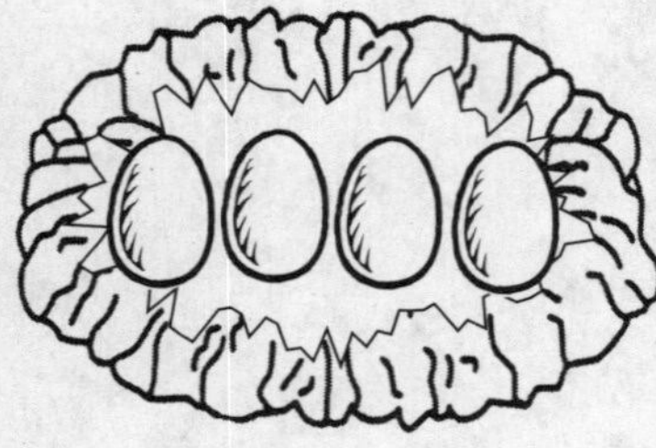 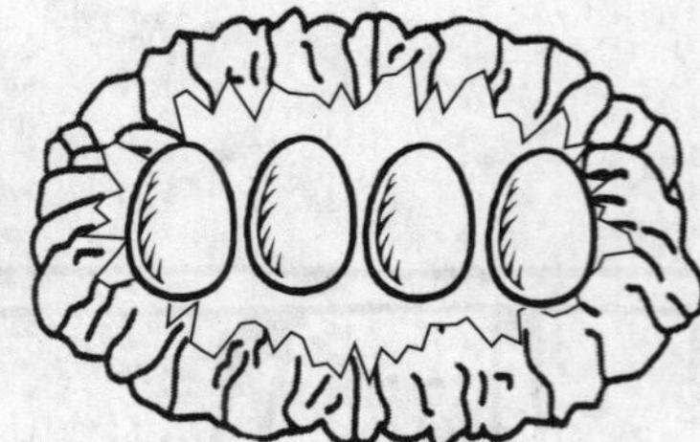 

______ and ______ ______

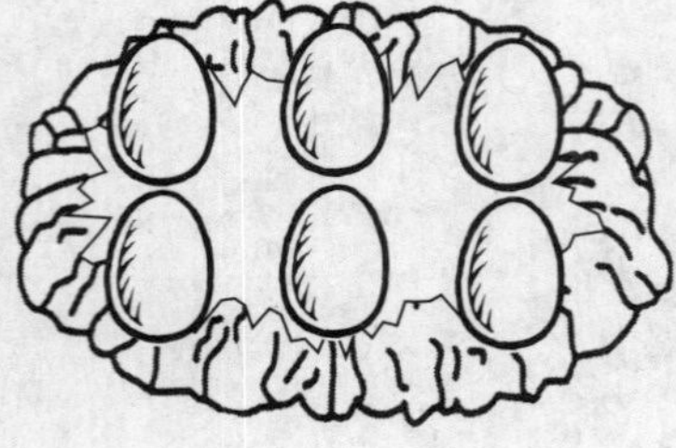 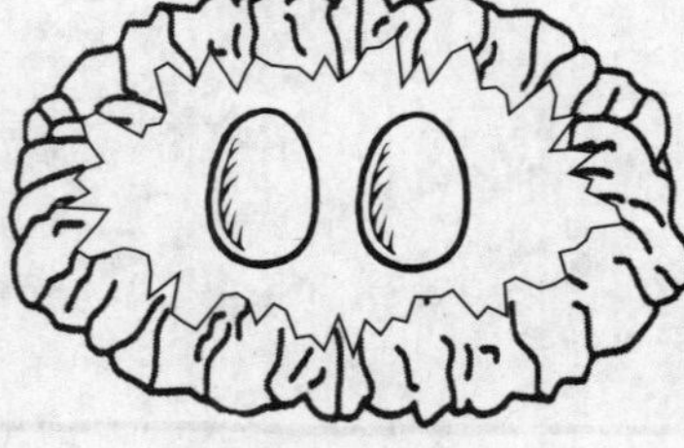 

______ and ______ ______

DIRECTIONS 1–2. Count and tell how many eggs are in each nest. Write the numbers. Draw that many eggs in the basket. Write the number.

Name ______________________________

Pick Up 8

COMMON CORE STANDARD CC.K.CC.3
Know number names and the count sequence.

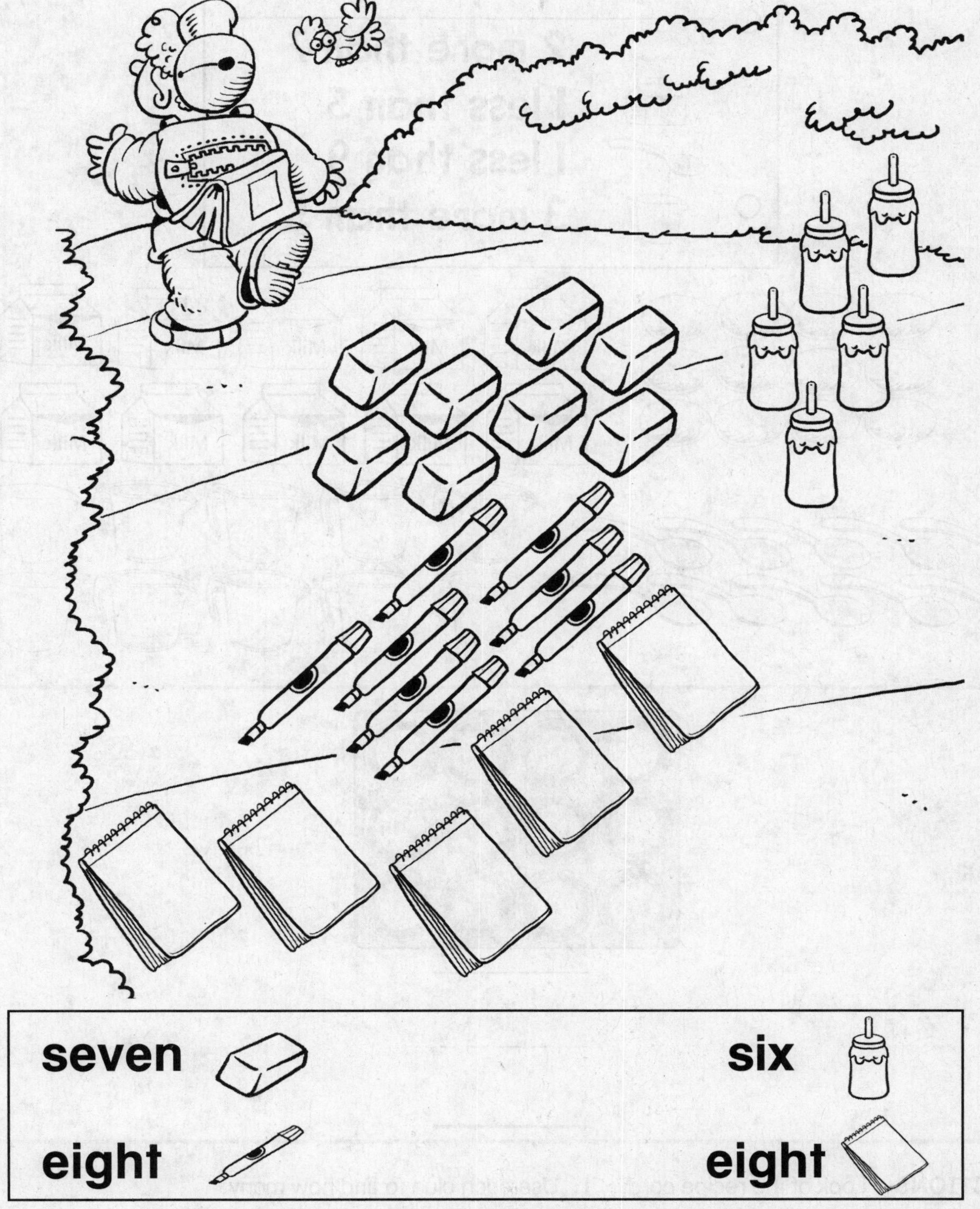

seven	**six**
eight	**eight**

DIRECTIONS Say the number words. Look at the big picture. Draw more objects or mark an X on some objects to match the number words.

Name ______________________

Bake with 9

COMMON CORE STANDARD CC.K.CC.5
Count to tell the number of objects.

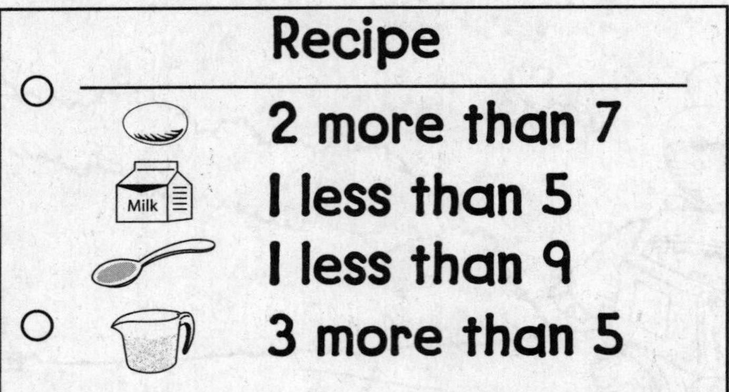

Recipe
2 more than 7
Milk
I less than 5
I less than 9
3 more than 5

1

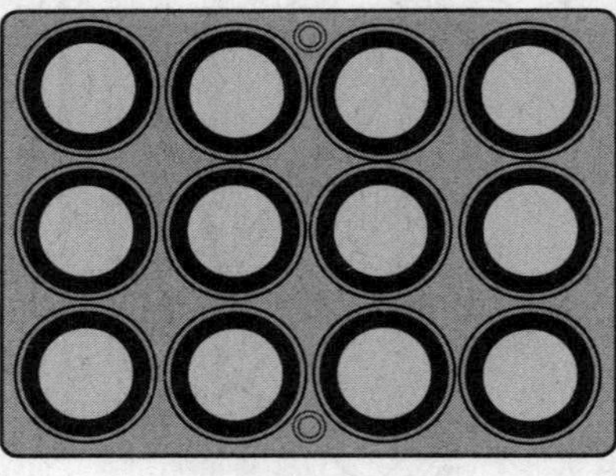

_____

DIRECTIONS Look at the recipe card. **1.** Use each clue to find how many: Two more than seven eggs, one less than five milks, one less than nine spoons, three more than five cups. Color that number of objects. **2.** Color five circles in the cupcake pan. Color four more. How many did you color in all? Write the number.

Name ____________________

COMMON CORE STANDARD CC.K.CC.3
Know number names and the count sequence.

After the Harvest

1

____________ **nine**

____________ **ten**

2

____________ **nine**

____________ **ten**

3

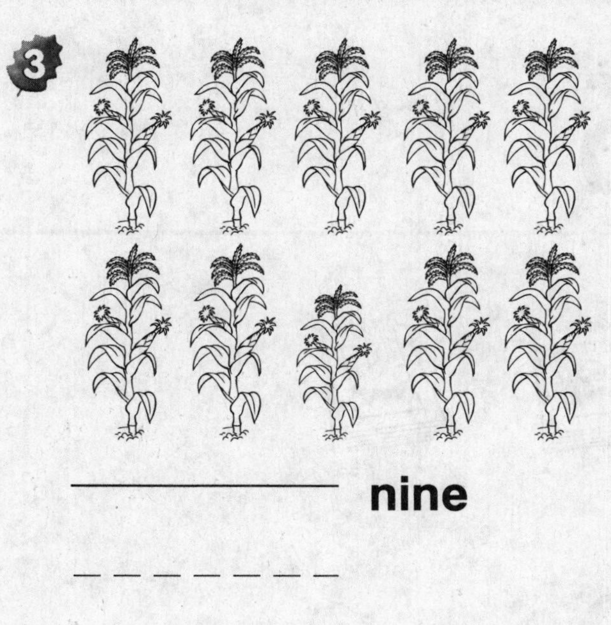

____________ **nine**

____________ **ten**

4

____________ **eight**

____________ **nine**

DIRECTIONS 1–4. Look at the set. Circle the object that is different. How many objects are the same? Count and circle the number word. Write how many.

Name ____________________________________

COMMON CORE STANDARD CC.K.CC.6
Compare numbers.

The Art of Numbers to 9

9

5

8

DIRECTIONS 1–3. Look at the art supplies. Draw more objects or mark an X on some if needed to match the number.

Name ____________________

COMMON CORE STANDARD CC.K.CC.5
Count to tell the number of objects.

Sets of 10

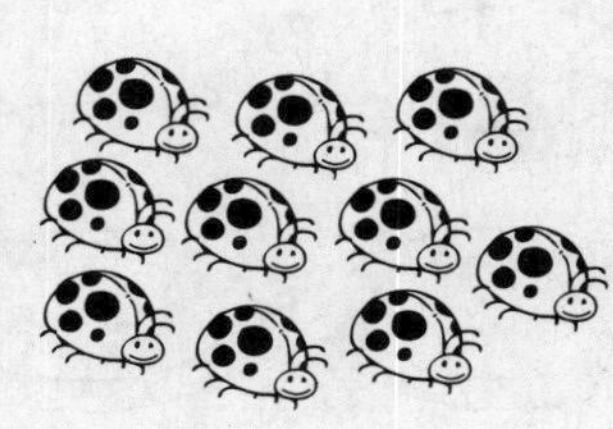
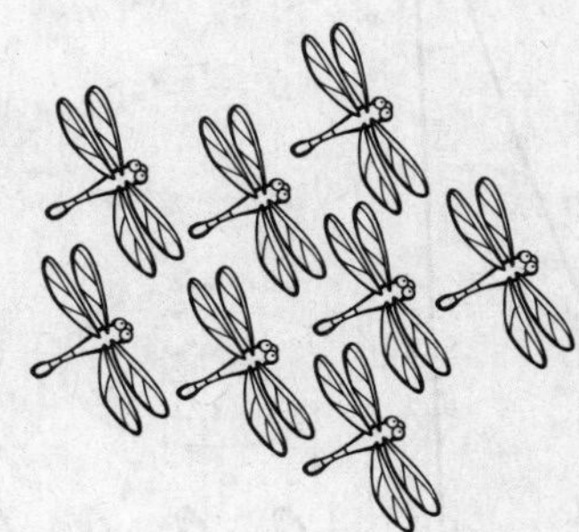

DIRECTIONS 1–3. Look for the set that has fewer than 10 objects. Mark an X through the set that does not have 10. Tell how many more are needed to make a set of 10.

Name ______________________________

Tabletop Ten

COMMON CORE STANDARD CC.K.CC.3
Know number names and the count sequence.

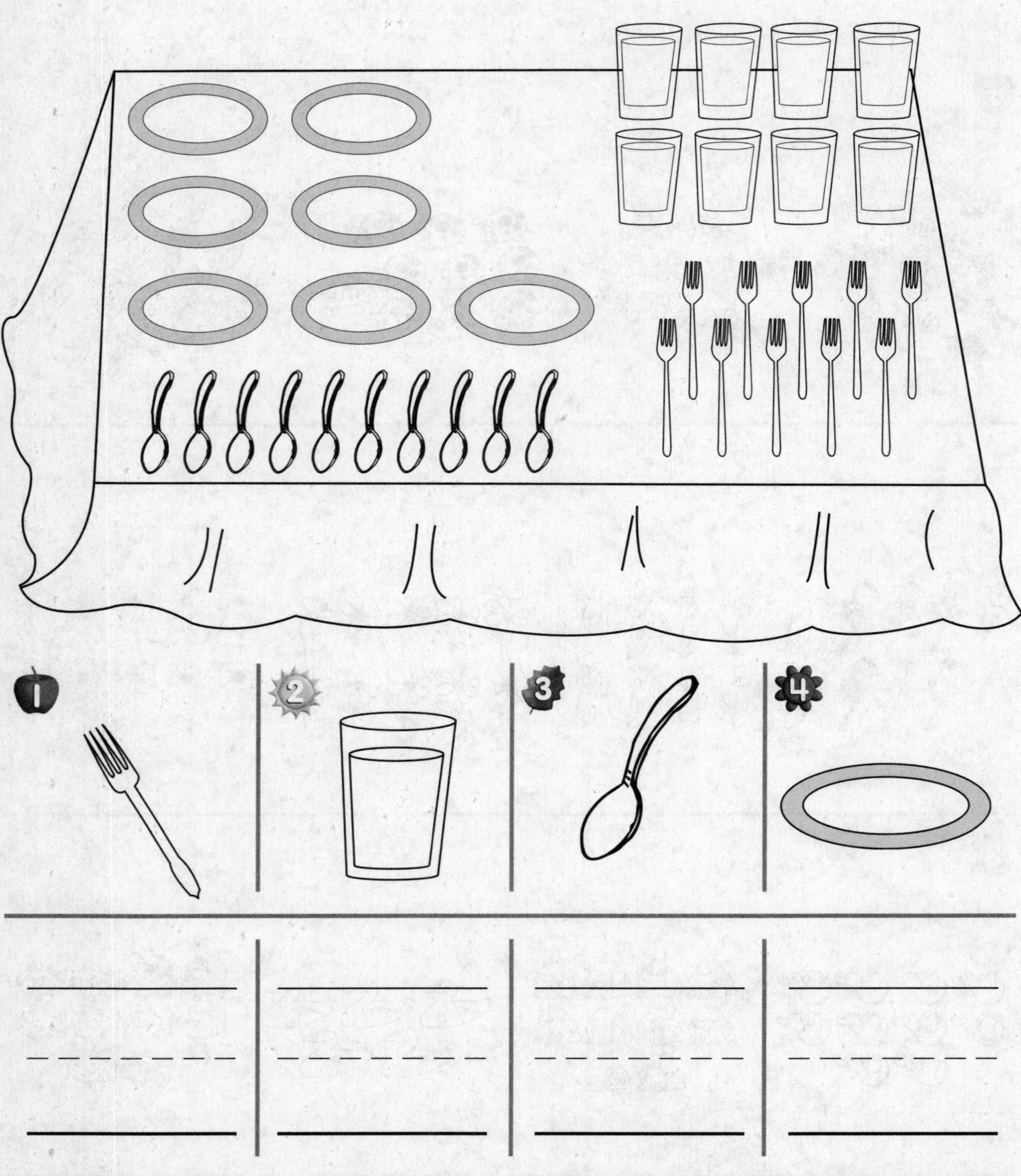

DIRECTIONS 1–4. Count and tell how many are in each set. Write the number. Circle the set that needs 3 more to have 10. Underline the set that needs 2 more to have 10.

Name ______________________________

Making 10

COMMON CORE STANDARD CC.K.OA.4
Understand addition as putting together and adding to, and understand subtraction as taking apart and taking from.

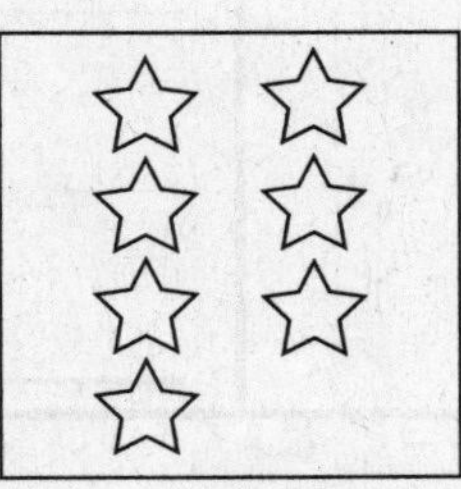

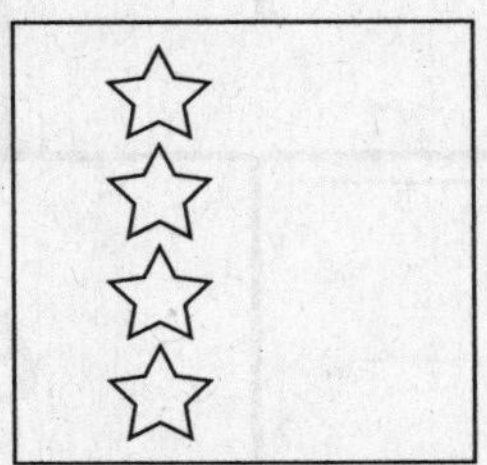

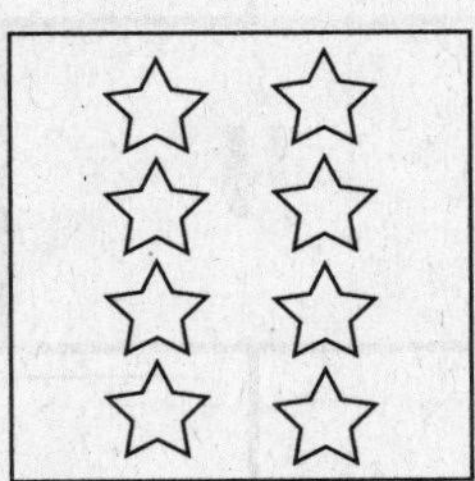

DIRECTIONS Make sets of 10. Draw a line to match each set of white stars with a set of gray stars to make 10. Name other ways to make 10.

Name ______________________

Missing Hopscotch

COMMON CORE STANDARD CC.K.CC.2
Know number names and the count sequence.

1

___	
2	3
4	
5	___
7	
___	9
10	

2

10	
8	___
7	
___	6
4	
2	___
1	

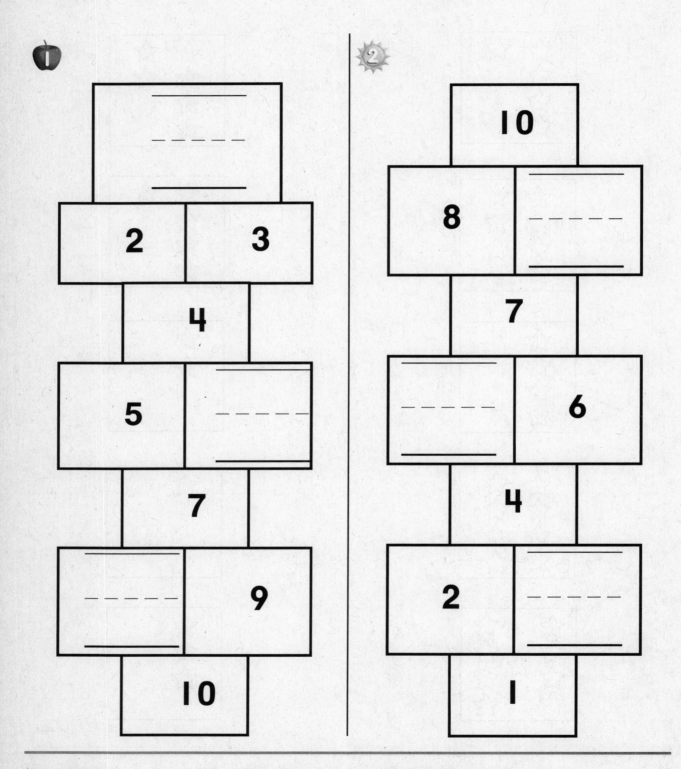

DIRECTIONS 1–2. Count in order. Write the numbers that fill the spaces.

Name ______________________

COMMON CORE STANDARD CC.K.CC.6
Compare numbers.

Sets of Nests

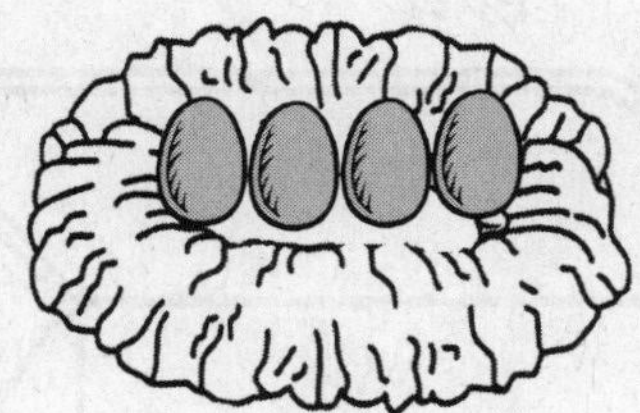

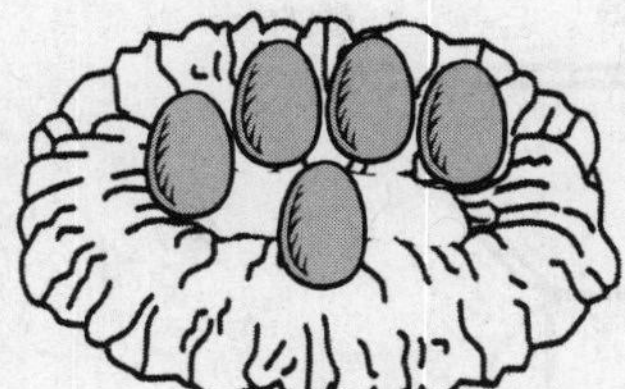

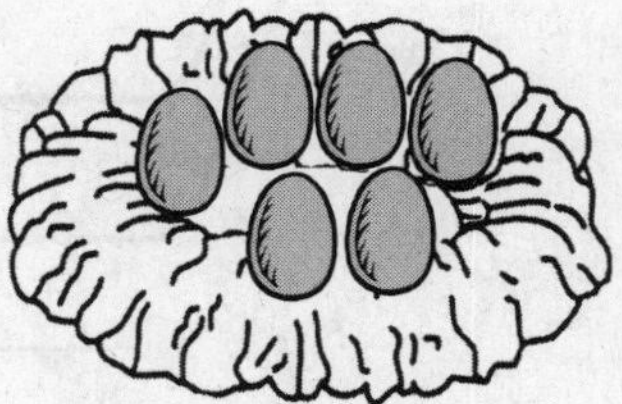

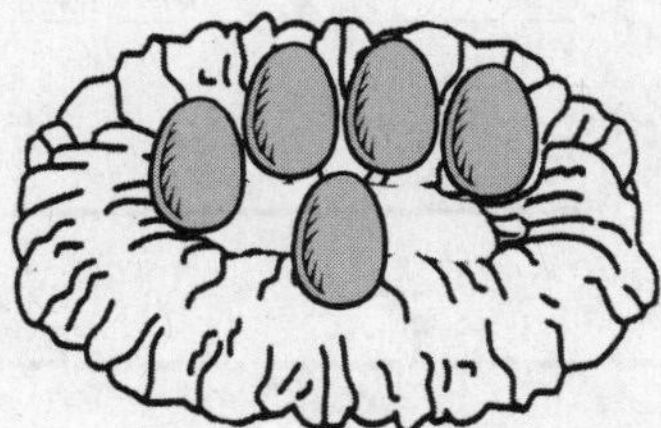

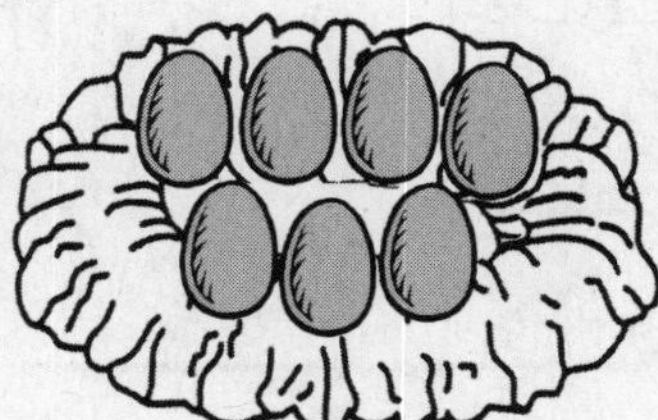

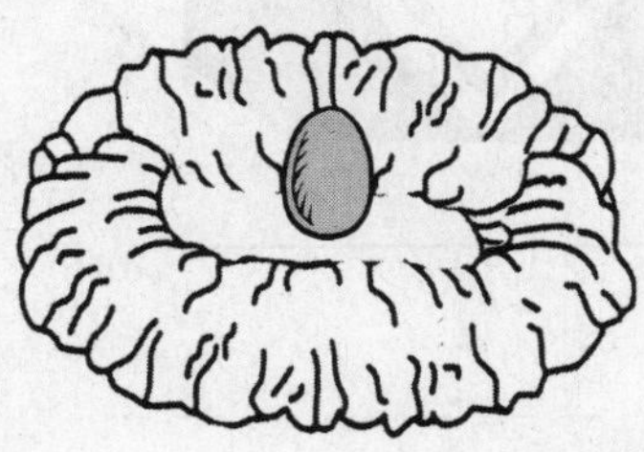

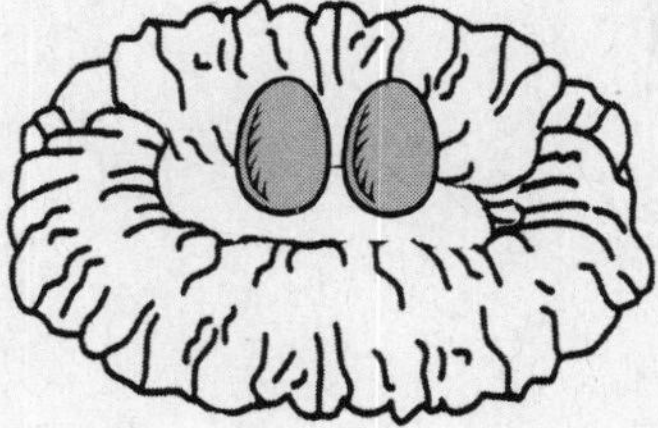

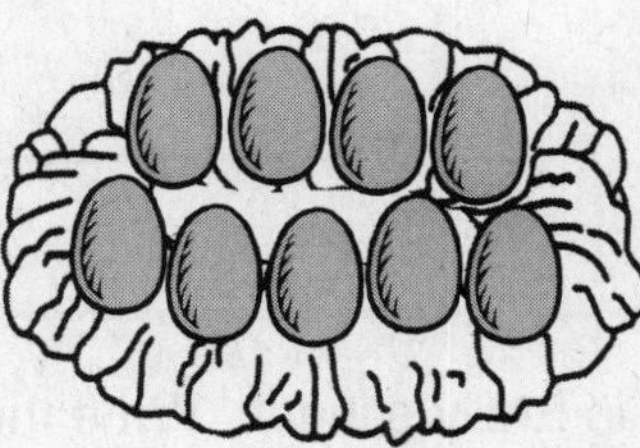

DIRECTIONS **1–3.** Count the eggs in each nest. Circle two nests so that there are 10 eggs in the two nests. Write the number of eggs in each nest that you circled.

Name ________________

COMMON CORE STANDARD CC.K.CC.6
Compare numbers.

Draw to Compare

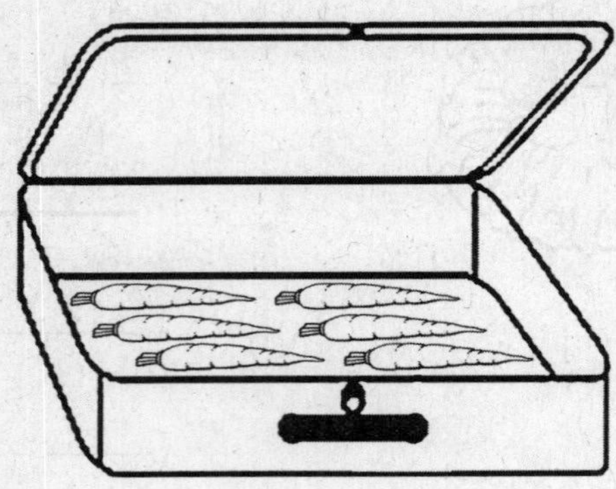

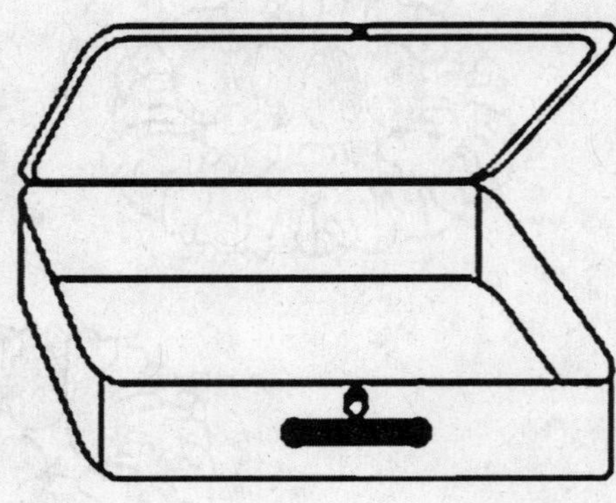

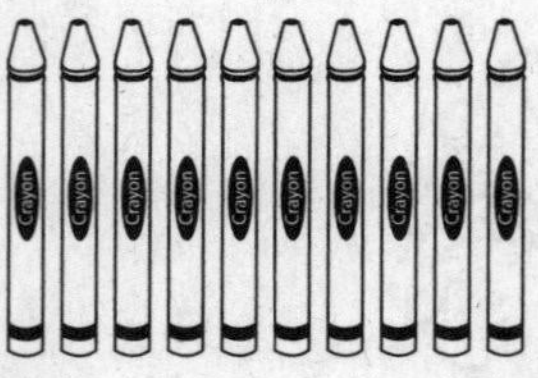

DIRECTIONS **1.** Count the number of carrots in Emily's lunch. Write the number. Jared has 8 carrots in his lunch. Draw Jared's carrots. Write the number. Circle the number that is greater. **2.** Count how many crayons Zak takes out of a box. Write the number. Janna takes 7 crayons out of a box. Draw Janna's crayons. Write the number. Circle the number that is less.

Name ______________________

COMMON CORE STANDARD CC.K.CC.7
Compare numbers.

How Many Marbles?

1

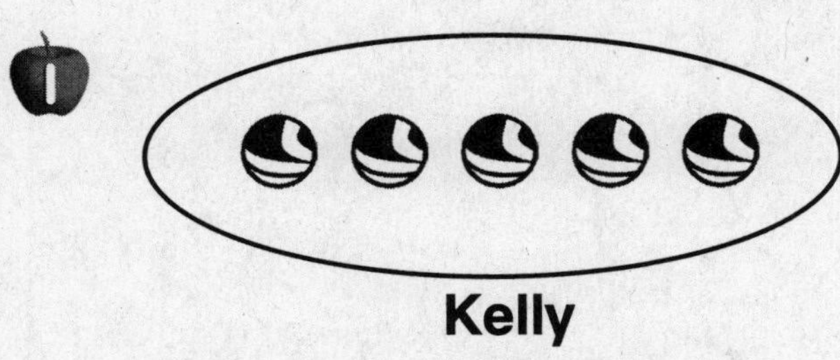

Kelly

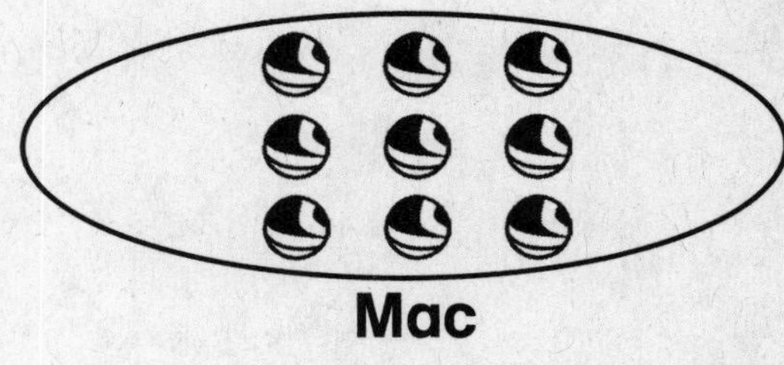

Mac

2

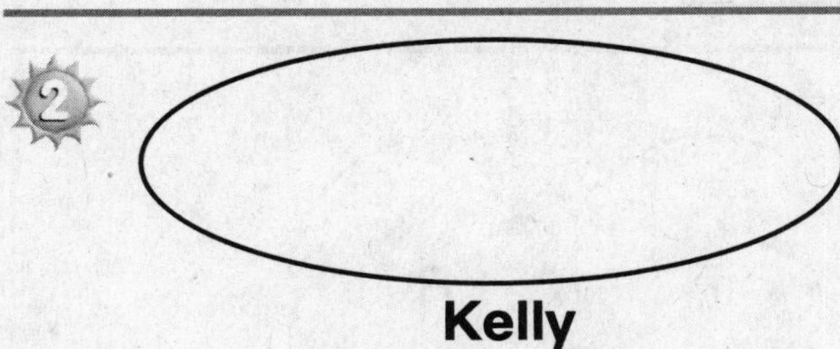

Kelly

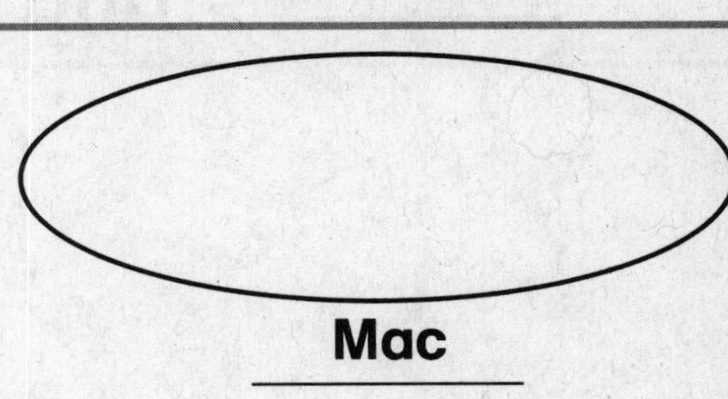

Mac

3

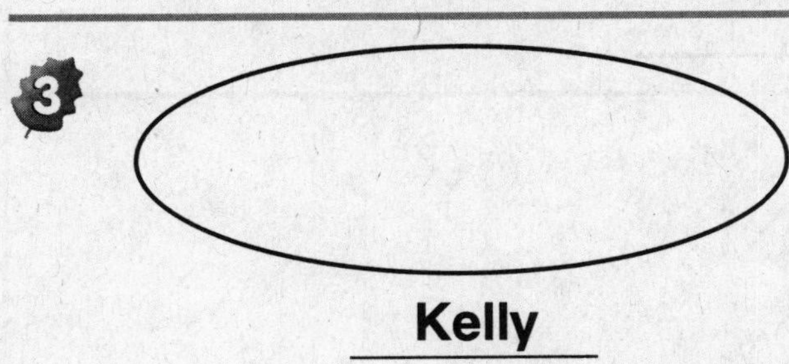

Kelly

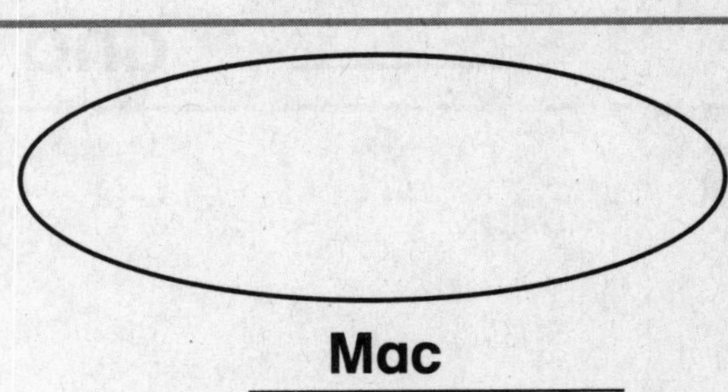

Mac

DIRECTIONS Kelly and Mac are playing marbles. **1.** Count the marbles that Kelly and Mac have. Write the numbers. Circle the greater number. **2.** Kelly wins 3 marbles from Mac. Draw pictures that show this. Write the numbers. Circle the greater number. **3.** Mac wins 4 marbles back from Kelly. Draw pictures that show this. Write the numbers. Circle the greater number.

Name ______________________________

COMMON CORE STANDARD CC.K.OA.1
Understand addition as putting together and adding to, and understand subtraction as taking apart and taking from.

Caterpillar Counters

1

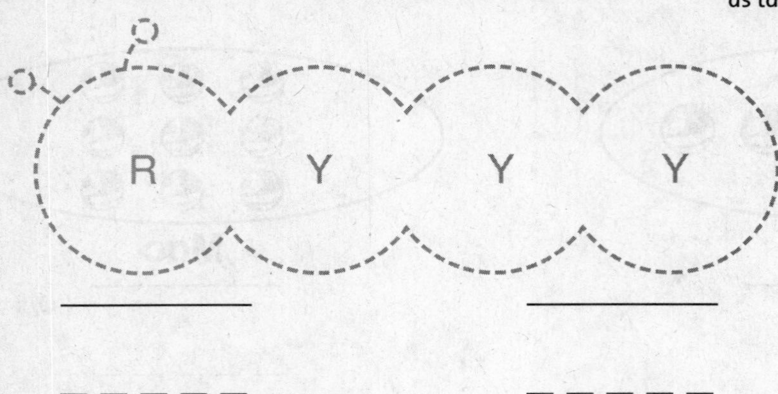

______ ______

______ and ______

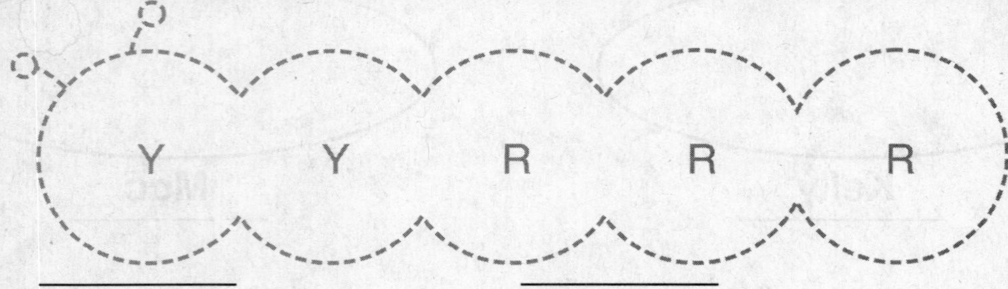

______ ______

______ and ______

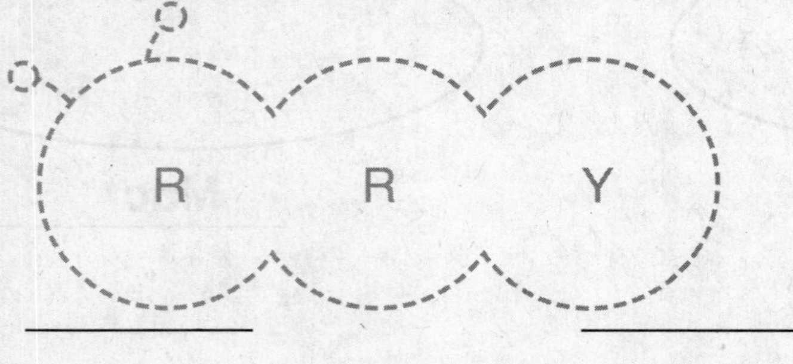

______ ______

______ and ______

DIRECTIONS 1–3. Place two-color counters as shown. R is for red, and Y is for yellow. How many of each color counter did you use? Write the numbers. Tell a friend how many counters are on the caterpillar now. Color the caterpillar to show the counters.

Name ______________________

Addition at the Beach

COMMON CORE STANDARD CC.K.OA.1
Understand addition as putting together and adding to, and understand subtraction as taking apart and taking from.

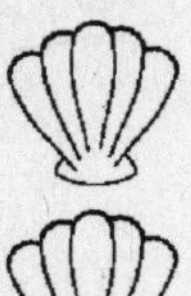

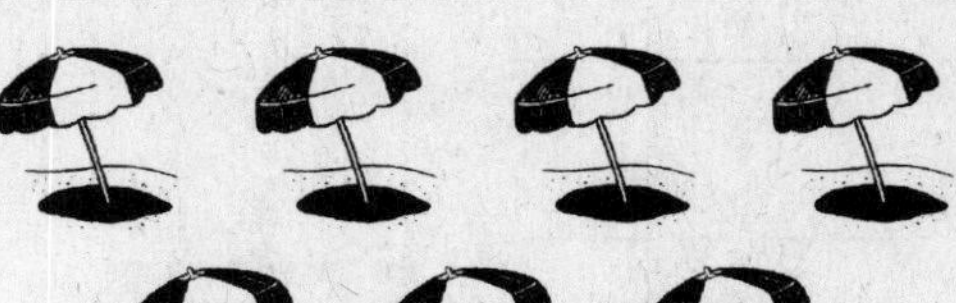

DIRECTIONS 1–3. Count and tell how many are in each set. Write the numbers and trace the symbol. Tell a friend how many there are in all.

Name ______________________

COMMON CORE STANDARD CC.K.OA.1
Understand addition as putting together and adding to, and understand subtraction as taking apart and taking from.

Fish Addition

1

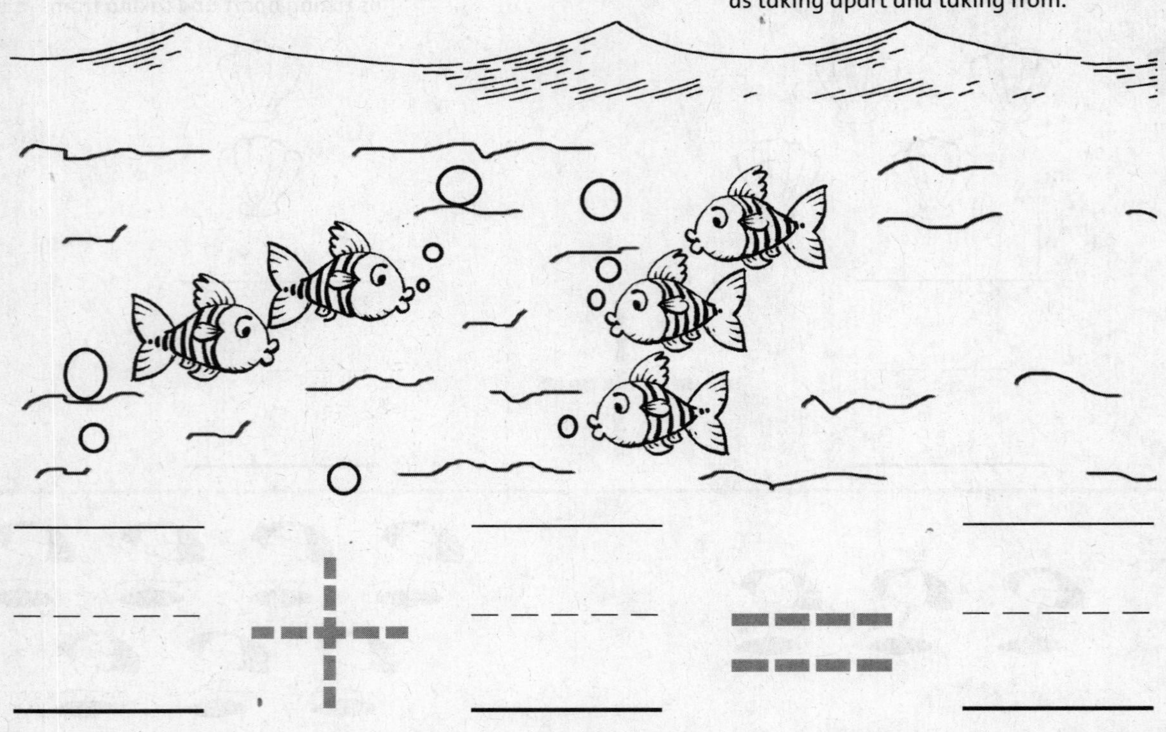

_____ + _____ = _____

2

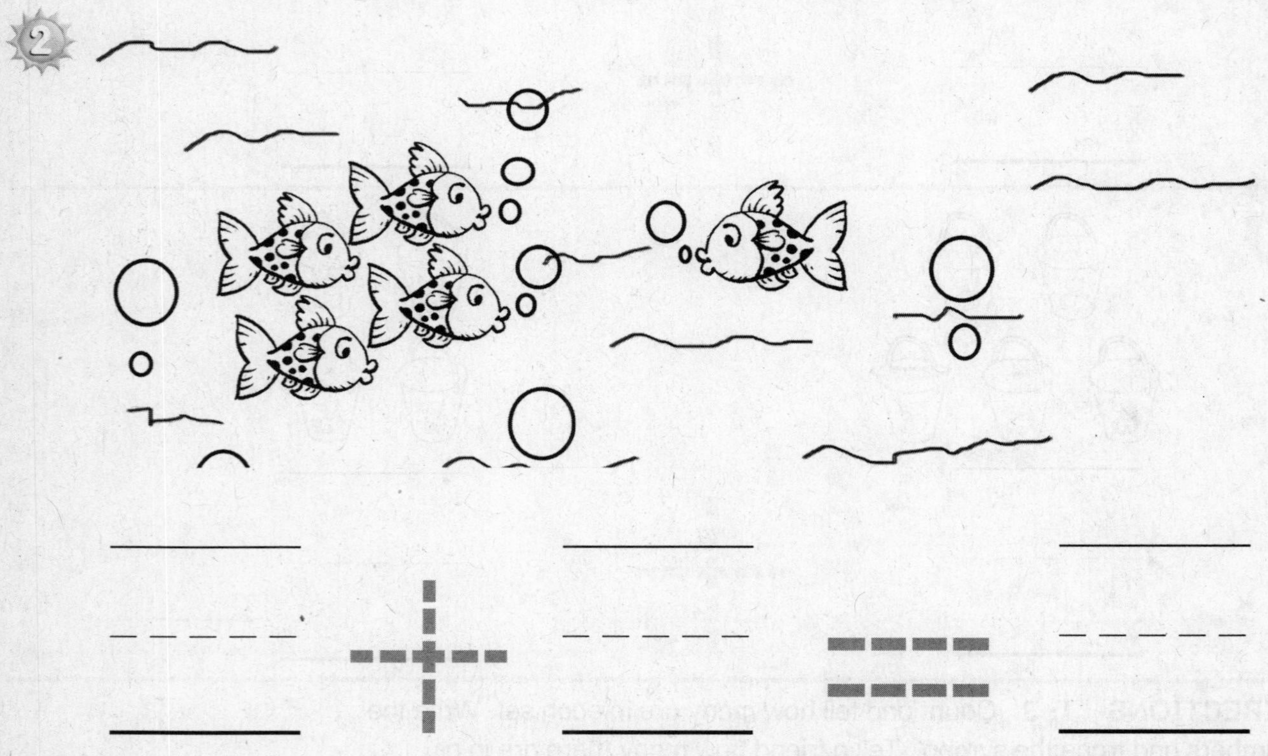

_____ + _____ = _____

DIRECTIONS 1–2. Count and write how many fish are in each set. Tell and write how many in all.

Name ______________________________

COMMON CORE STANDARD CC.K.OA.5
Understand addition as putting together and adding to, and understand subtraction as taking apart and taking from.

Adding Up Flowers

DIRECTIONS **1.** Color some of the flower red. Color the rest of the flowers blue. Write how many of each color. Complete the addition sentence to show how many in all. **2.** Draw 4 flowers in the vase. Color some of the flowers yellow. Color the rest of the flowers orange. Write how many of each color. Complete the addition sentence to show how many in all.

Name ______________________

Draw and Count

COMMON CORE STANDARD CC.K.OA.4
Understand addition as putting together and adding to, and understand subtraction as taking apart and taking from.

8 + ____ = 10

7 + ____ = 10

6 + ____ = 10

DIRECTIONS **1–3.** Draw ten balloons. Look at the first number. Color that many balloons red. Color the rest of the balloons blue. How many balloons did you color blue? Write the number. Trace the symbols to complete the addition sentence.

Name ________________________

COMMON CORE STANDARD CC.K.OA.5
Understand addition as putting together and adding to, and understand subtraction as taking apart and taking from.

How Many in All?

7

8

9

4

5

6

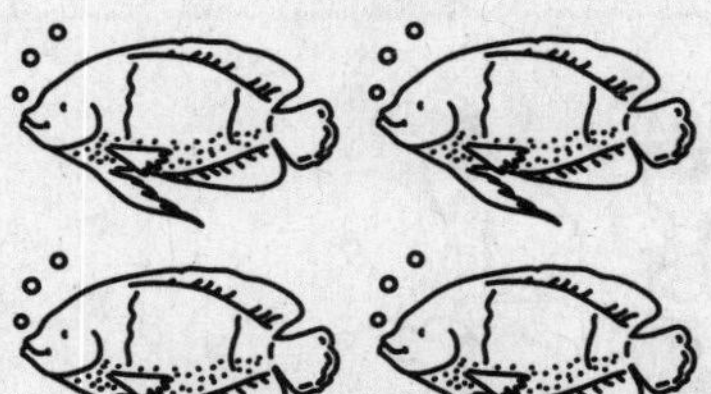

8

9

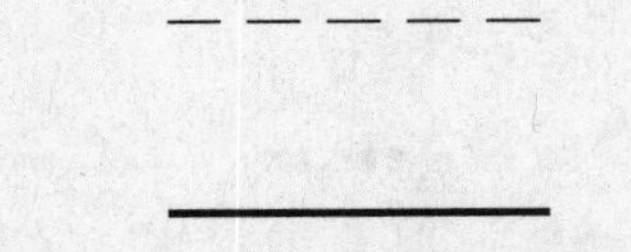

10

DIRECTIONS I–3. Write how many are in each set. Trace the symbol. Circle the number that shows how many in all.

Name ________________

COMMON CORE STANDARD CC.K.OA.2
Understand addition as putting together and adding to, and understand subtraction as taking apart and taking from.

Pet Store Addition

1

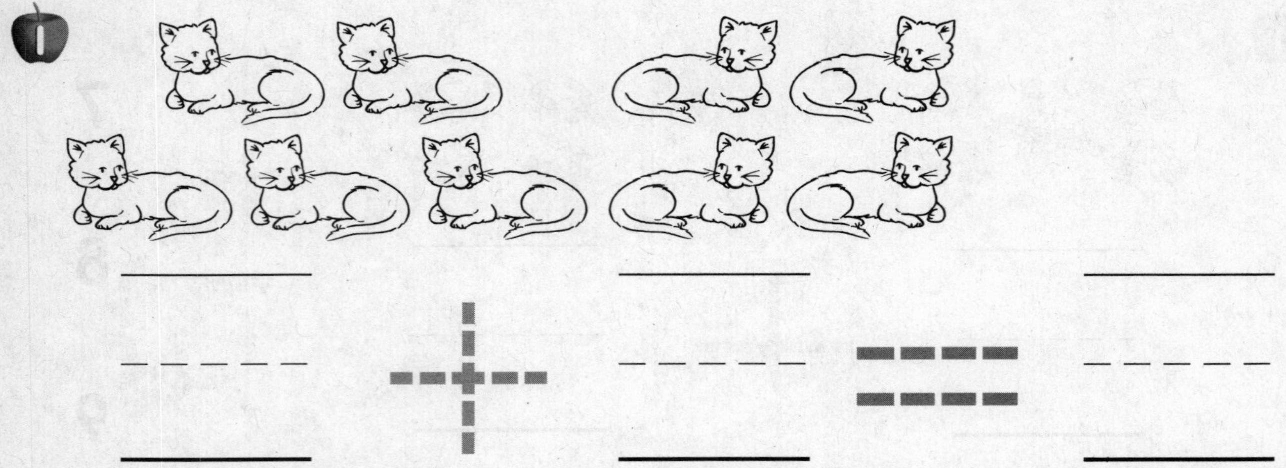

2

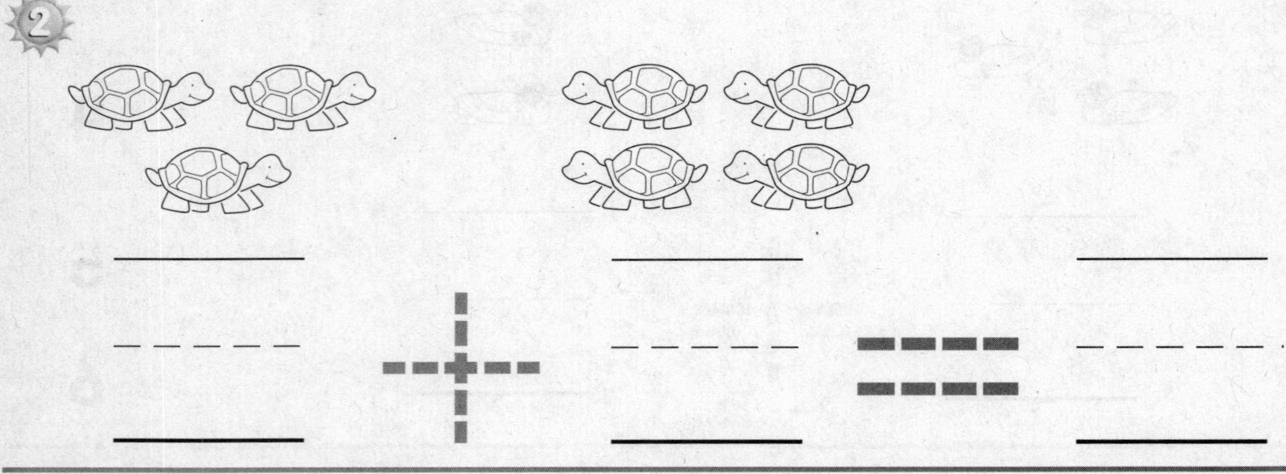

3

DIRECTIONS 1–3. Look at the two sets of animals. Complete the addition sentence to show that one set is being added to the other.

Name ______________________

COMMON CORE STANDARD CC.K.OA.3

Understand addition as putting together and adding to, and understand subtraction as taking apart and taking from.

5 in the Hive

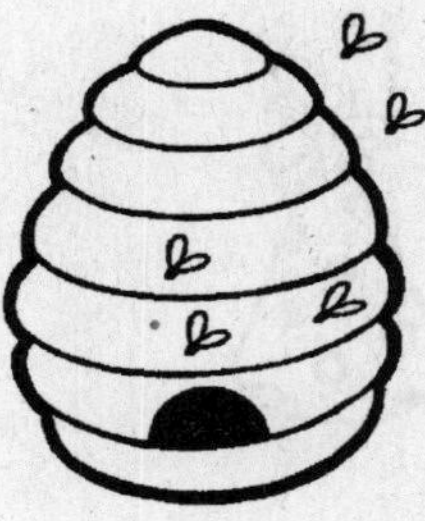

5 = ____ + ____

5 = ____ + ____

5 = ____ + ____

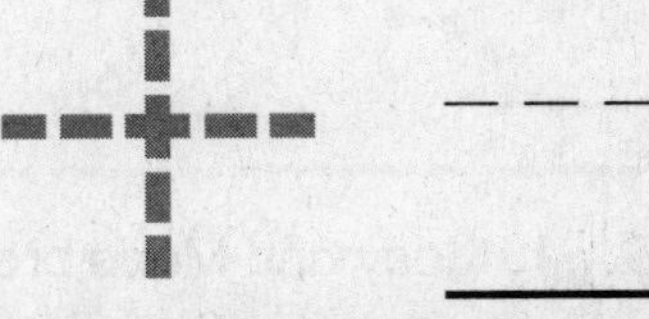

DIRECTIONS **1–3.** How many bees are on the hive? How many bees are outside the hive? Write an addition sentence to show a pair of numbers that makes 5.

Name ____________________

Lesson 5.9
Enrich

Addition Party

COMMON CORE STANDARD CC.K.OA.3
Understand addition as putting together and adding to, and understand subtraction as taking apart and taking from.

    ____

2

7  ____

 ____  ____

DIRECTIONS **1.** Joey and Maria brought 6 party hats. Joey brought 4 party hats. Draw Maria's party hats. Complete the addition sentence. **2.** Jenny and Will brought 7 balloons. Jenny brought 5 balloons. Draw Will's balloons. Complete the addition sentence. **3.** Tracey and Maribel brought 7 apples. Tracey brought 3 apples. Draw Maribel's apples. Write the addition sentence.

Name ____________________

Picnic for 8

COMMON CORE STANDARD CC.K.OA.3
Understand addition as putting together and adding to, and understand subtraction as taking apart and taking from.

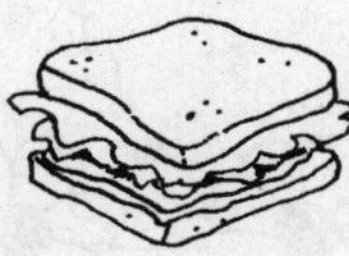

8 = 5 + ___

8 = 4 + ___

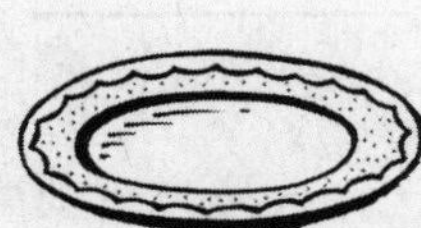

8 = ___ + ___

DIRECTIONS Eight friends are having a picnic. They do not have enough of everything they need. **1–3.** Count the objects in each set. How many more do the friends need? Draw enough to make 8. Complete the addition sentences to show the number pair that makes 8.

Name ___________________________

Daisy Chains

COMMON CORE STANDARD CC.K.OA.3
Understand addition as putting together and adding to, and understand subtraction as taking apart and taking from.

9 = 3 + ___

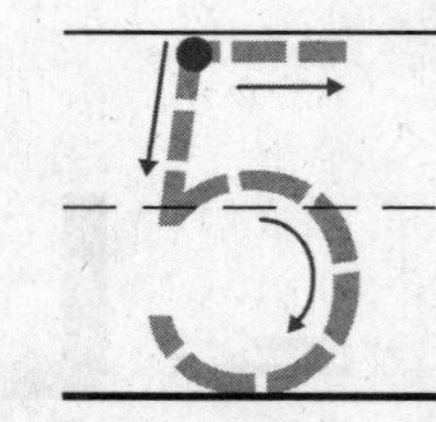

9 = 5 + ___

9 = 2 + ___

DIRECTIONS **1–3.** Trace the number. Color that many daisies yellow. Then color the rest of the daisies orange. How many daisies are orange? Write the number to show a number pair for 9.

Name ______________________

COMMON CORE STANDARD CC.K.OA.3
Understand addition as putting together and adding to, and understand subtraction as taking apart and taking from.

Add Beads

1

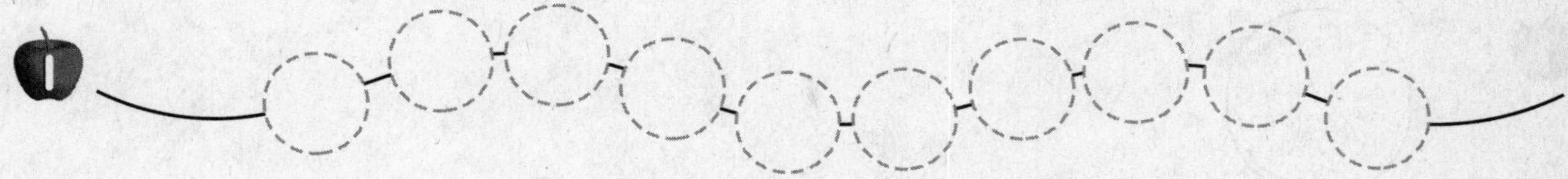

10 = ____ + ____

2

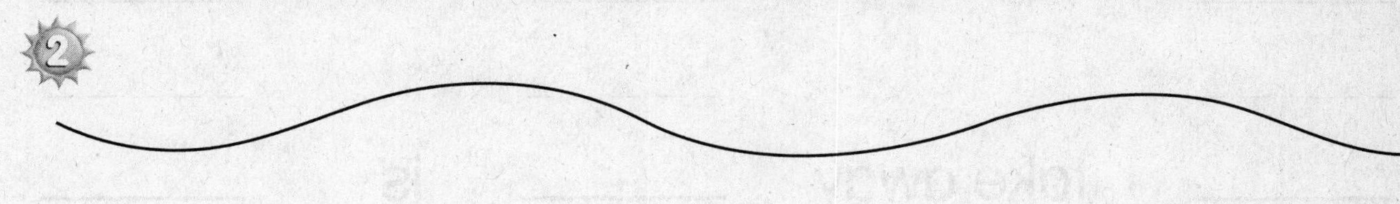

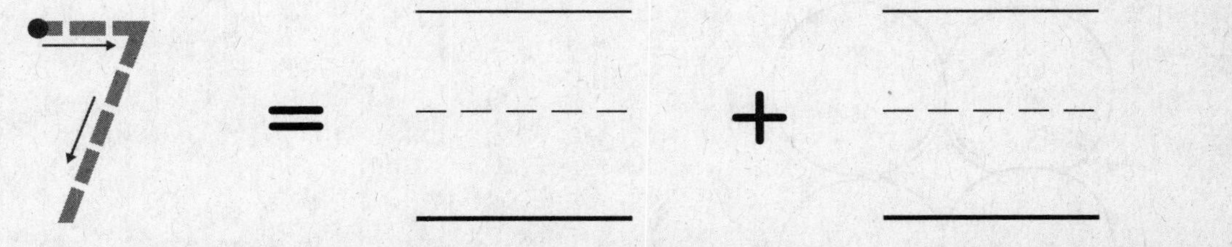

7 = ____ + ____

3

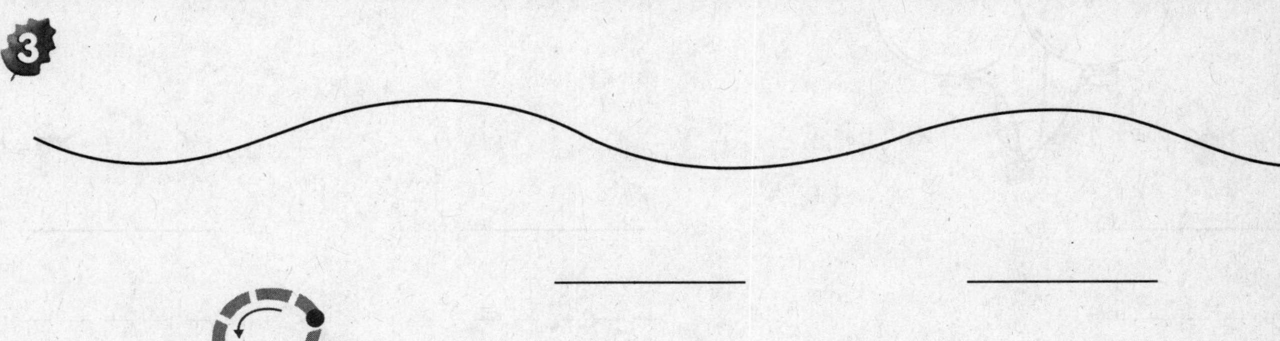

9 = ____ + ____

DIRECTIONS 1–3. Trace the number. Trace or draw that many beads. Color some beads blue. Then color the rest of the beads green. Count and write how many of each color bead to show a number pair.

Name ________________________

COMMON CORE STANDARD CC.K.OA.1
Understand addition as putting together and adding to, and understand subtraction as taking apart and taking from.

Take Away Balloons

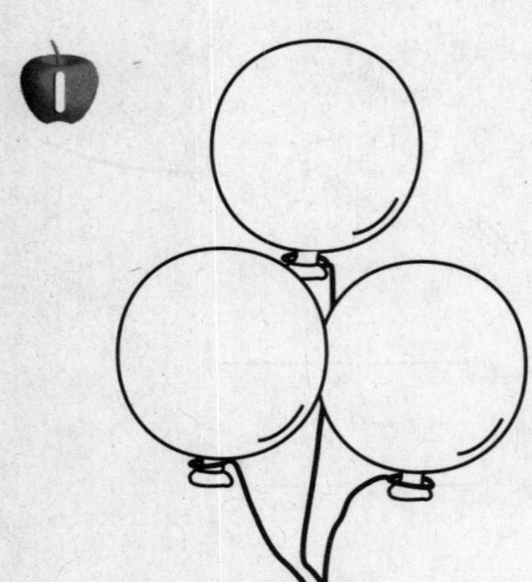

______ take away ______ is ______.

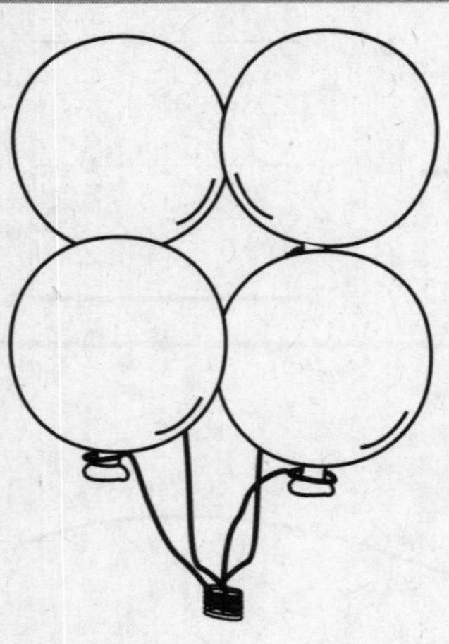

______ take away ______ is ______.

DIRECTIONS **1–2.** Tell a subtraction word problem. Draw to show some balloons flying away. Write the numbers to show the subtraction.

Name ______________________

Bead Subtraction

COMMON CORE STANDARD CC.K.OA.1
Understand addition as putting together and adding to, and understand subtraction as taking apart and taking from.

1

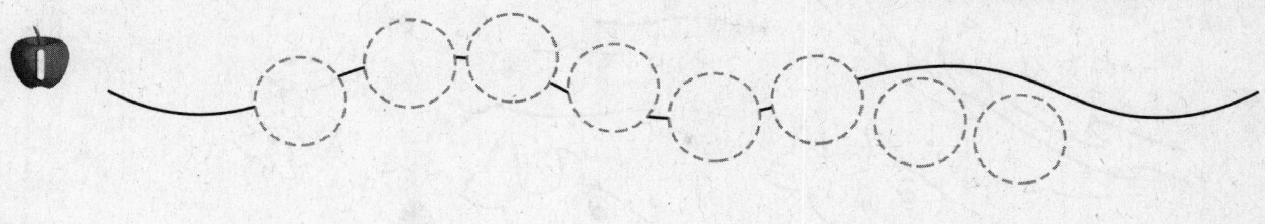

______ − ______ = ______

2

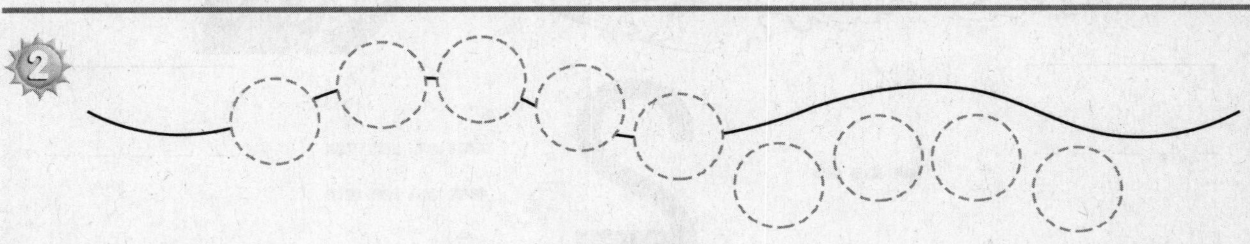

______ − ______ = ______

3

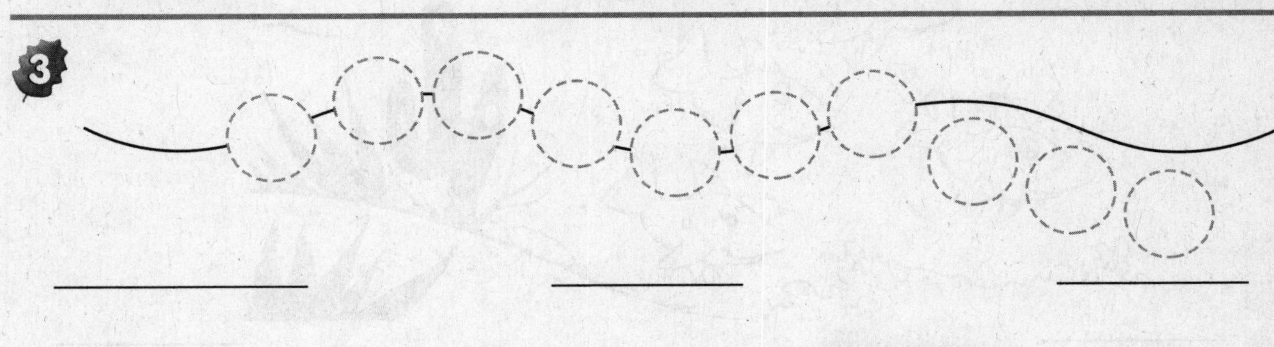

______ − ______ = ______

DIRECTIONS 1–3. Tell a subtraction word problem. Color the beads on the string one color. Color the beads that have fallen off another color. Complete the subtraction sentence to show the problem.

Name ____________________

Shark Subtraction

COMMON CORE STANDARD CC.K.OA.1
Understand addition as putting together and adding to, and understand subtraction as taking apart and taking from.

1

____ − 2 = ____

2

____ − 3 = ____

DIRECTIONS 1-2. Tell a subtraction word problem about the fish. Circle the fish that are swimming away. Write the numbers and trace the symbols to complete the subtraction sentence.

Name ______________________

Subtraction Stories

COMMON CORE STANDARD CC.K.OA.5
Understand addition as putting together and adding to, and understand subtraction as taking apart and taking from.

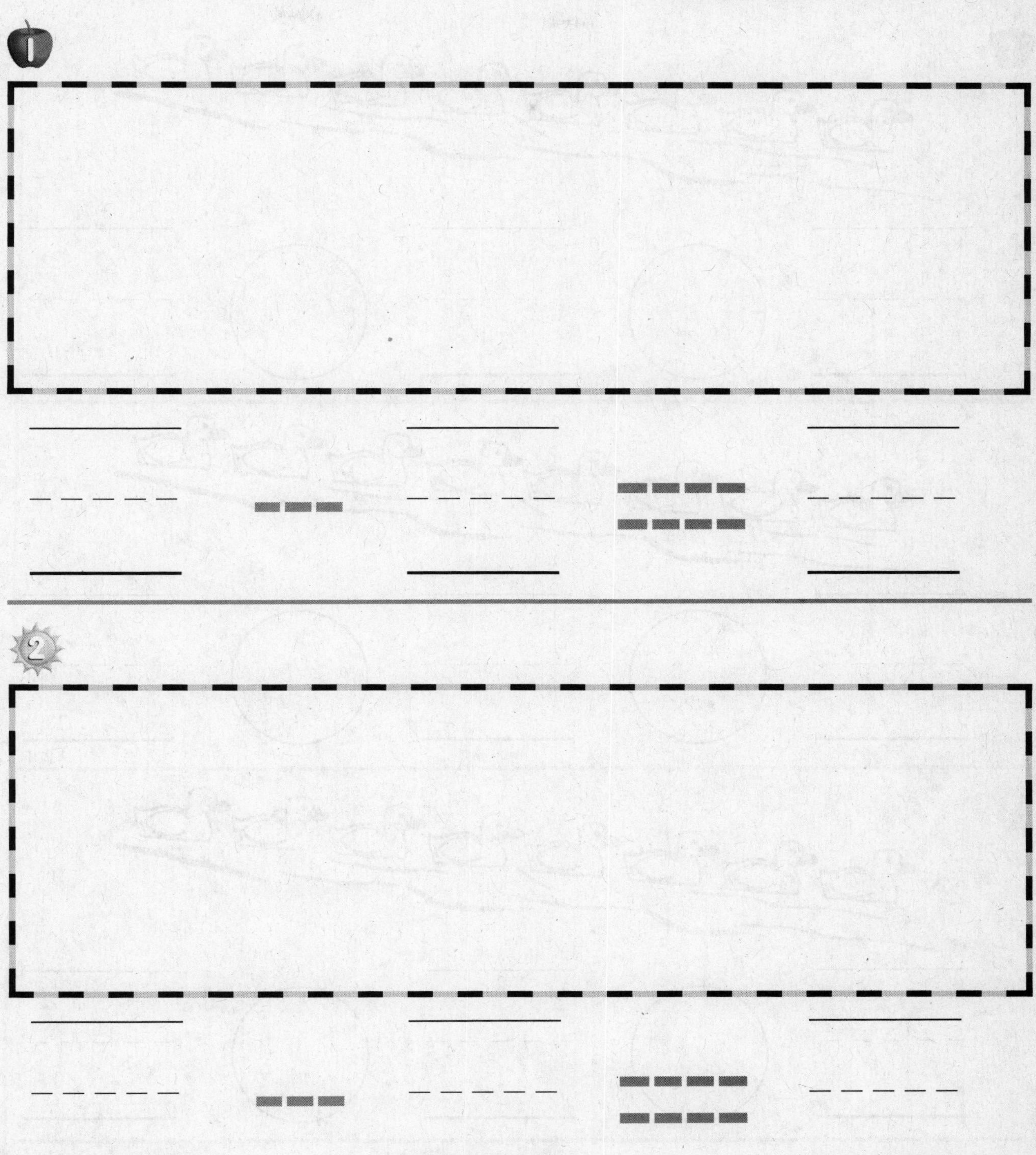

DIRECTIONS 1–2. Tell a subtraction word problem about cubes. Draw the cube train. Model to show the cube train being taken apart. Draw the cube train parts. Write the subtraction sentence for your word problem.

Name ______________________

Duck Subtraction

COMMON CORE STANDARD CC.K.OA.5
Understand addition as putting together and adding to, and understand subtraction as taking apart and taking from.

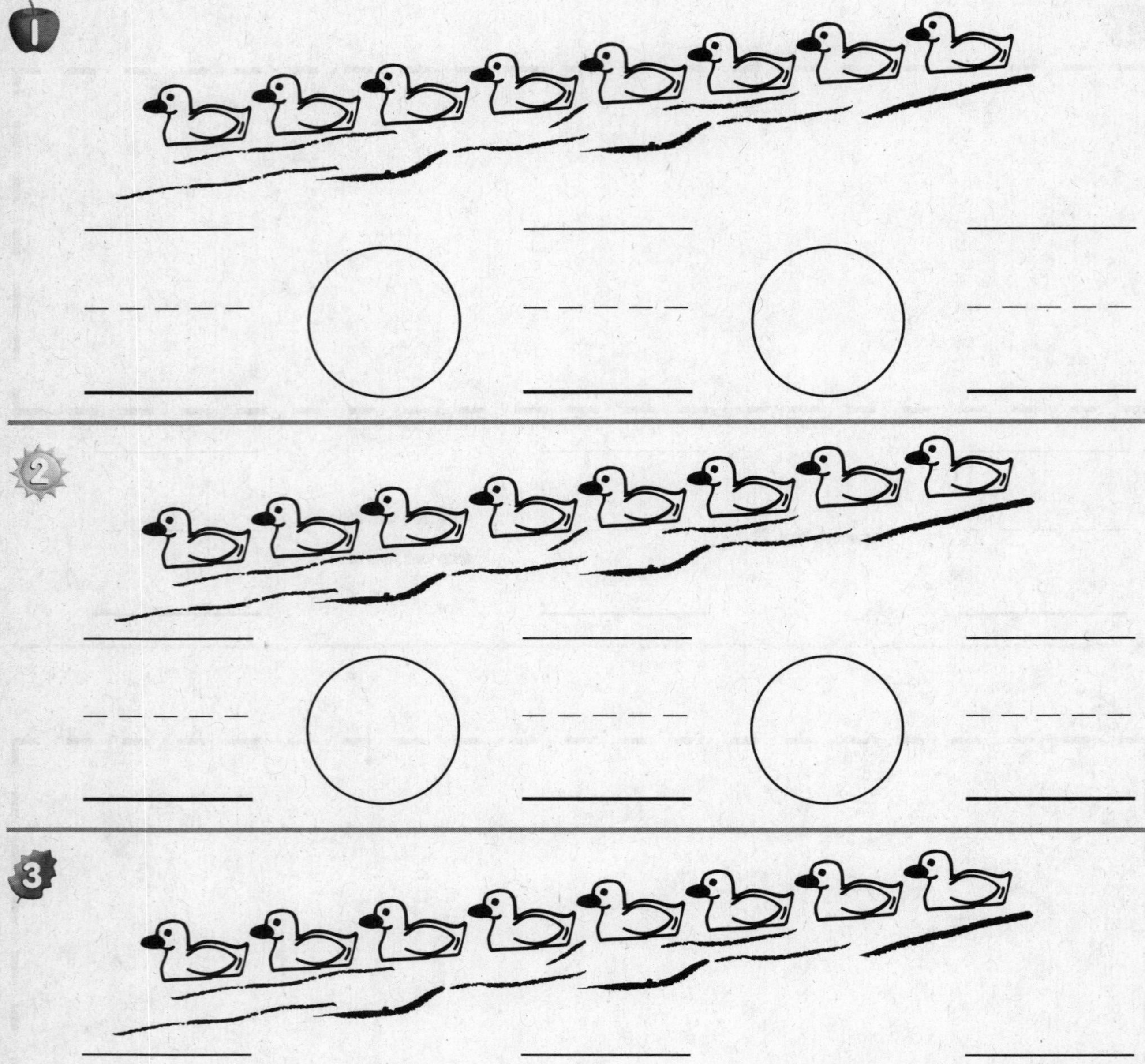

DIRECTIONS 1. Tell a subtraction word problem. Circle and mark an X to show how many are being taken from the set. Write the subtraction sentence. 2–3. Tell a different subtraction word problem. Circle and mark an X to show how many are being taken from the set. Write the subtraction sentence.

Name ____________________

Draw and Subtract

COMMON CORE STANDARD CC.K.OA.2
Understand addition as putting together and adding to, and understand subtraction as taking apart and taking from.

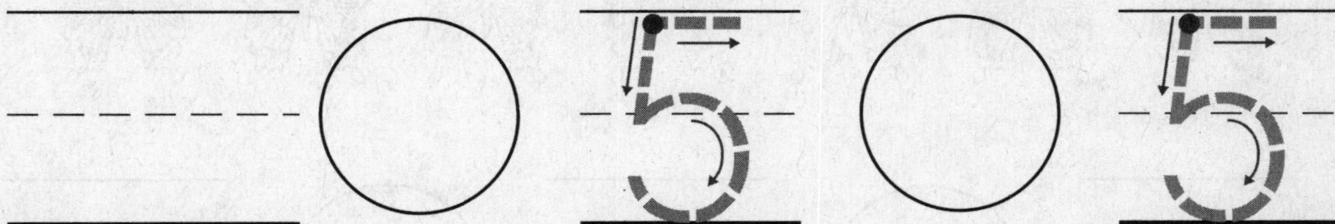

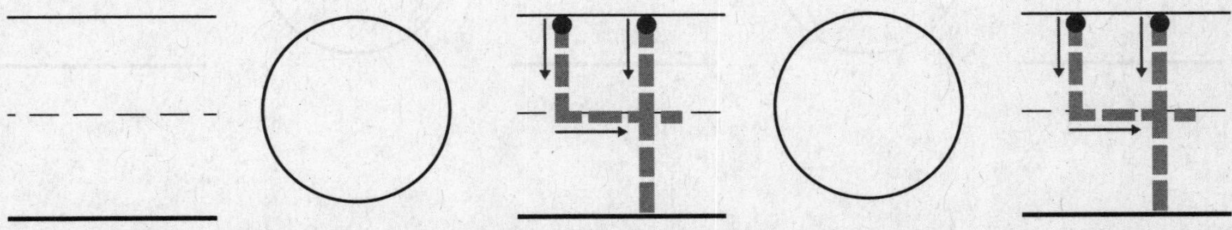

DIRECTIONS **1–3.** Tell a subtraction word problem about objects. Draw objects to show how many you started with. Circle and make an X on the objects being taken from the set. Write and trace to complete the subtraction sentence.

Name ____________________

Addition or Subtraction

COMMON CORE STANDARD CC.K.OA.2
Understand addition as putting together and adding to, and understand subtraction as taking apart and taking from.

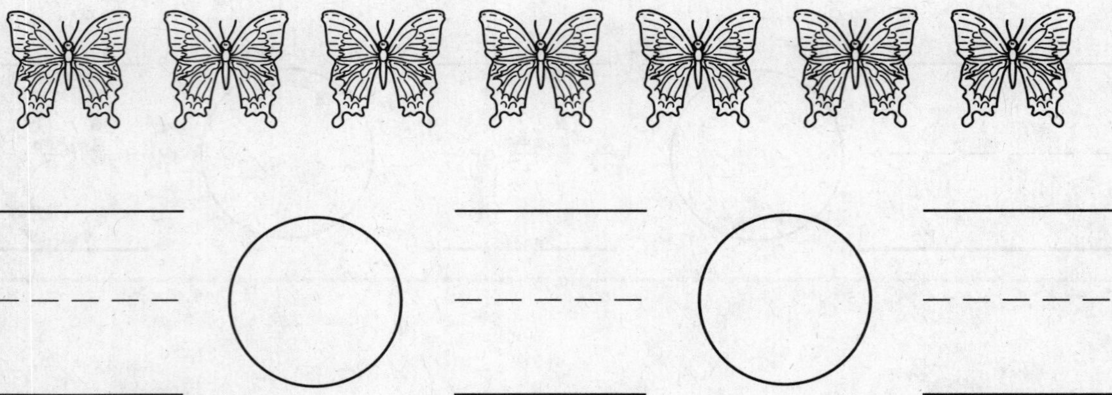

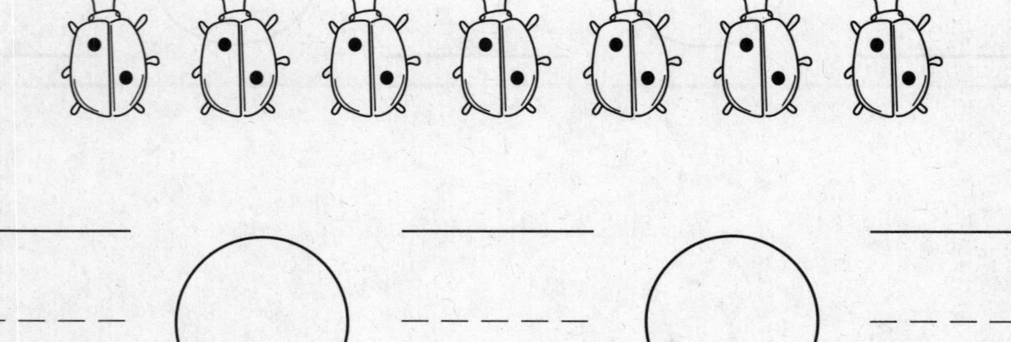

DIRECTIONS: **1.** Tell a word problem about the butterflies. Write the number sentence. **2.** Tell a word problem about the ladybugs. Write the number sentence.

Name ______________________

COMMON CORE STANDARD CC.K.NBT.1
Work with numbers 11–19 to gain foundations for place value.

Which Two Sets?

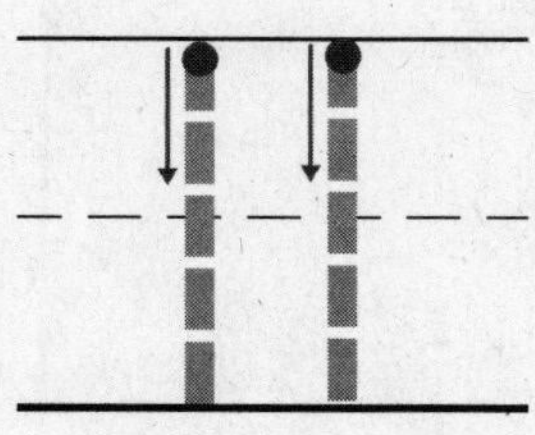

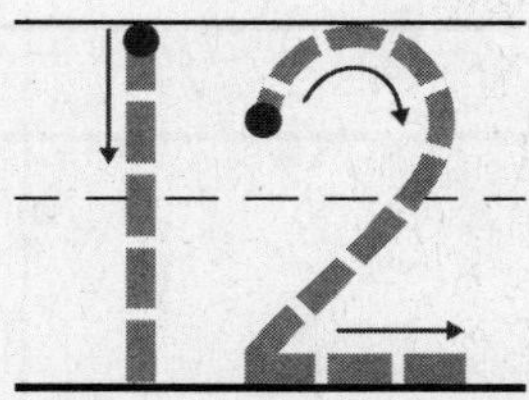

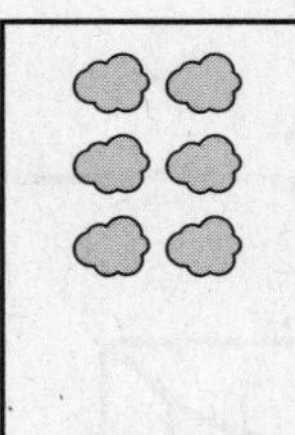

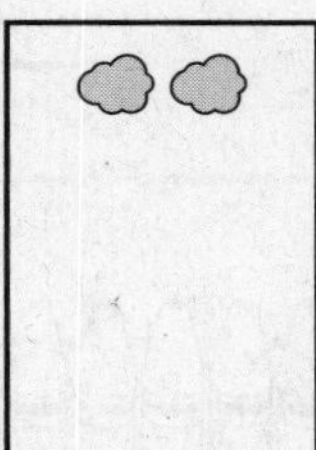

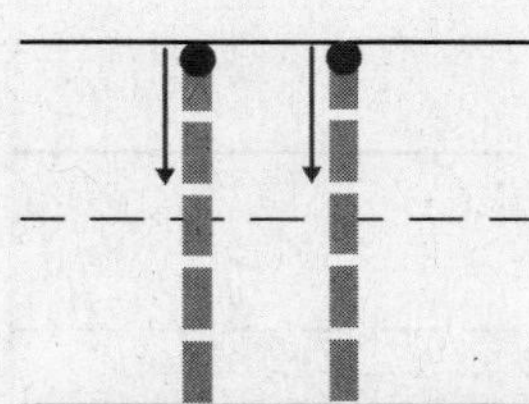

DIRECTIONS **1–3.** Trace the number. Circle the two sets that make the number.

Name ______________________

COMMON CORE STANDARD CC.K.CC.3
Know number names and the count sequence.

Fill the Crayon Boxes

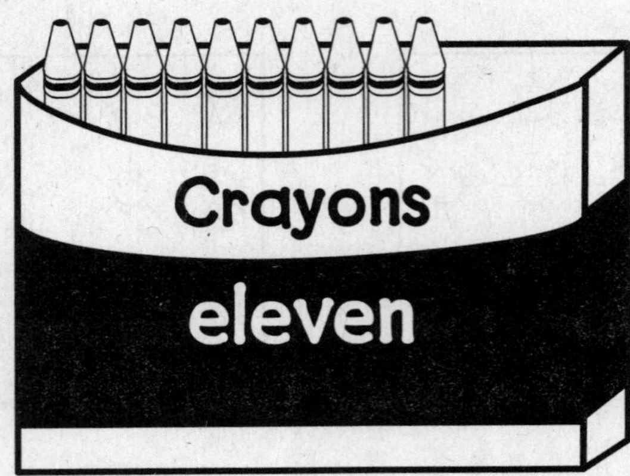

___ + ___ = ___

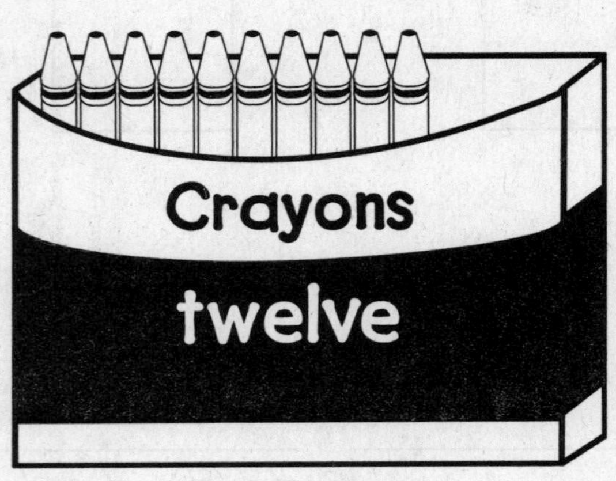

___ + ___ = ___

DIRECTIONS 1–2. Count the crayons. Write the number. Say the number word on the box. Draw some more crayons to match the number word. How many did you draw? Look at the crayons you counted and the crayons you drew. Complete the addition sentence to match.

Name ____________________

Show 13 and 14 Waffles

COMMON CORE STANDARD CC.K.NBT.1
Work with numbers 11–19 to gain foundations for place value.

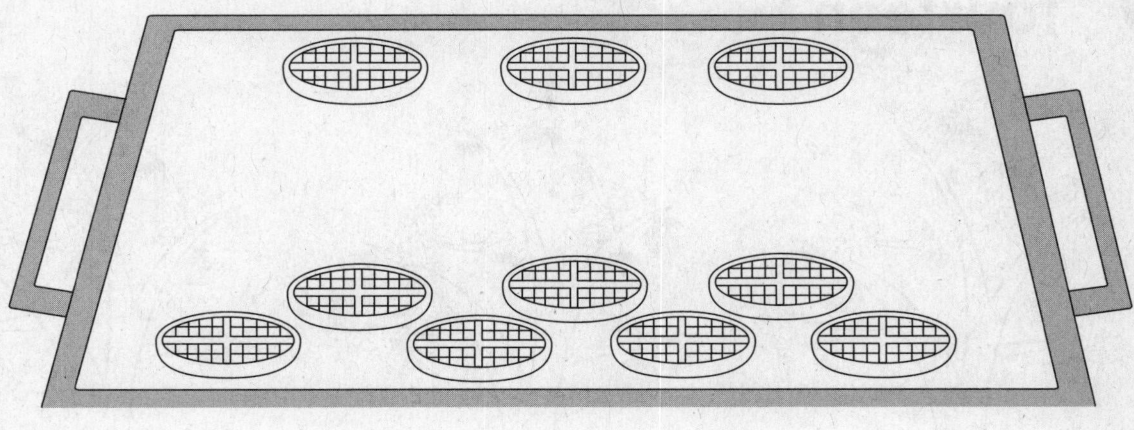

_______ waffles and _______ waffles

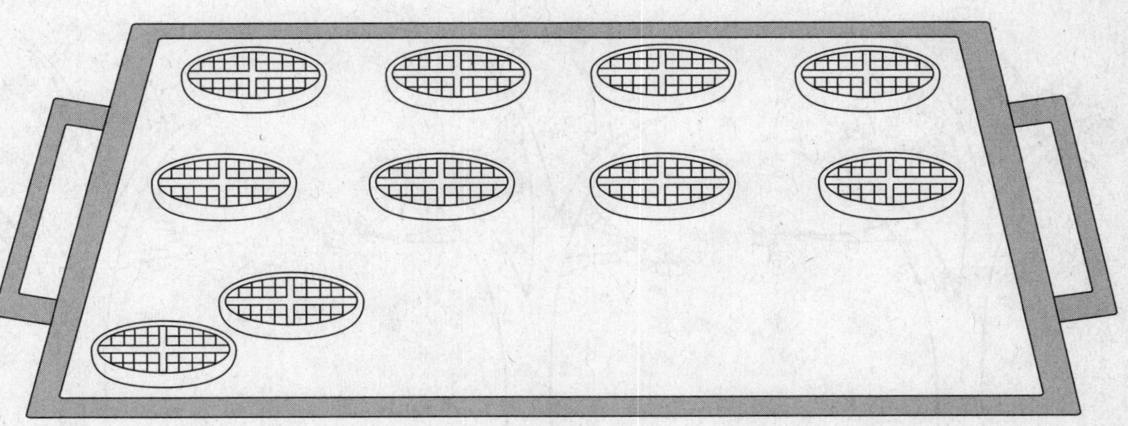

_______ waffles and _______ waffles

DIRECTIONS **1.** How many waffles are on the platter? Write the number. Draw more waffles to show 13. How many waffles did you draw? Write the number. **2.** How many waffles are on the platter? Write the number. Draw more waffles to show 14. How many waffles did you draw? Write the number.

Name ____________________

Garden with 13 and 14

COMMON CORE STANDARD CC.K.CC.3
Know number names and the count sequence.

1 fourteen

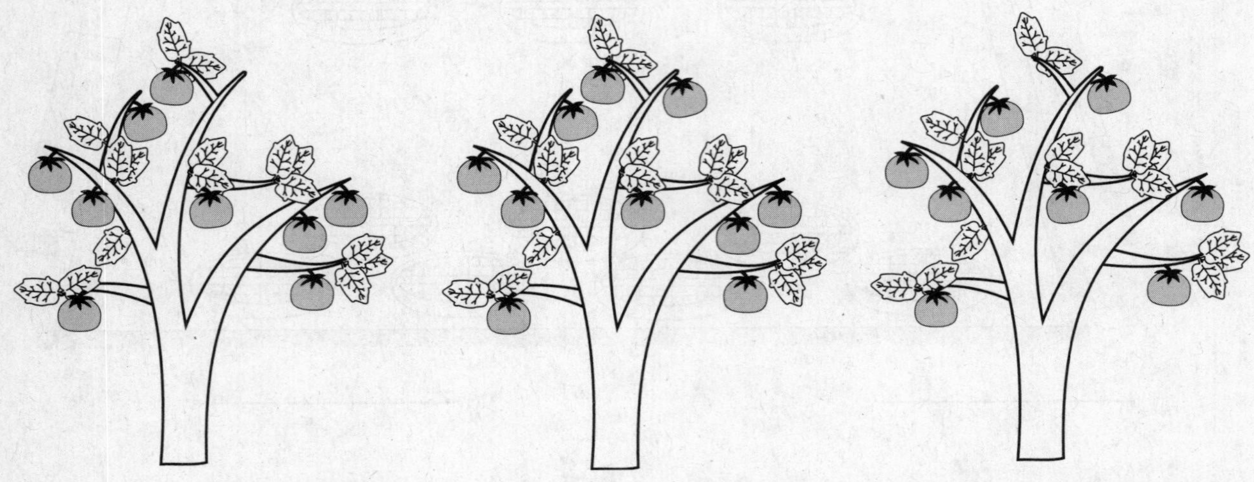

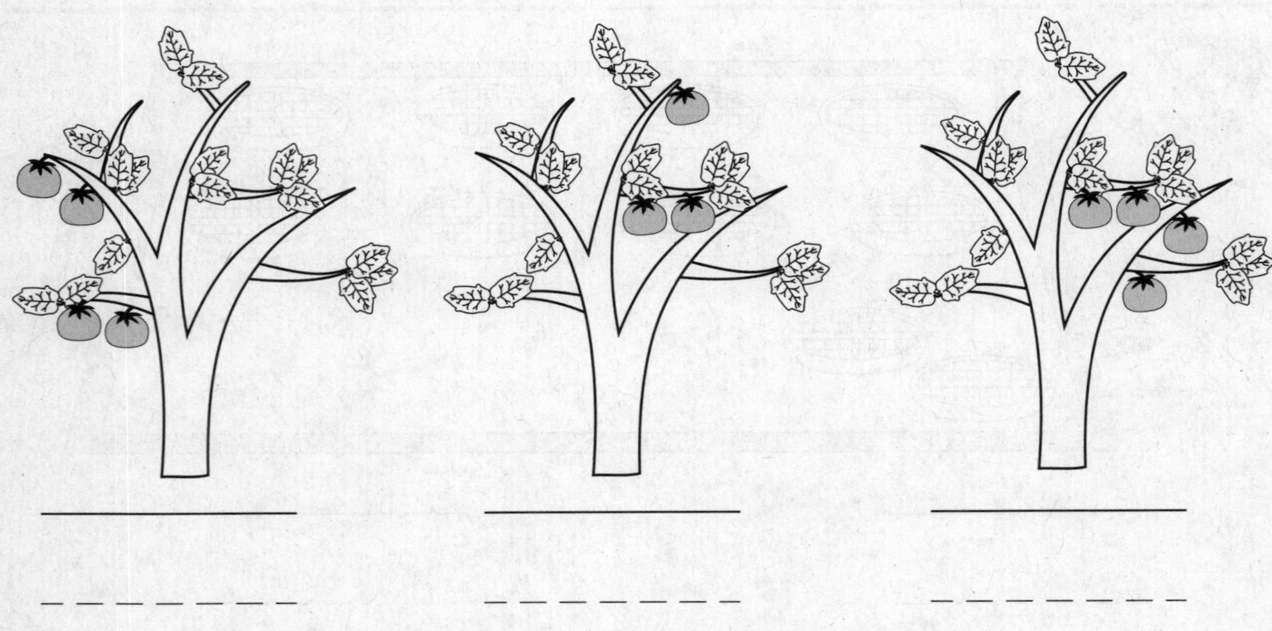

DIRECTIONS 1. Say the number word. Circle the plant that needs four more tomatoes to match the number word. 2. Draw 10 more tomatoes on each plant. Count and write how many.

Name ______________________

15 Sunflower Petals

COMMON CORE STANDARD CC.K.NBT.1
Work with numbers 11–19 to gain foundations for place value.

10

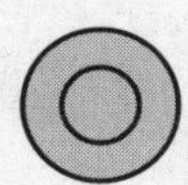

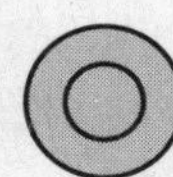

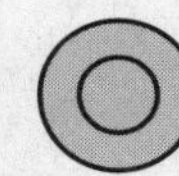

DIRECTIONS Each set of sunflowers needs 15 petals in all. **1.** Draw petals on the second flower. Write how many you drew. **2–3.** Draw petals on each flower. Write how many you drew. Use different numbers each time.

Name ______________________

COMMON CORE STANDARD CC.K.CC.3
Know number names and the count sequence.

Seating Chart

1

2

_______ girls _______ boys

DIRECTIONS **1.** Mr. Lee has 15 children in his class. They sit in two rows. The top row has one more child than the bottom row. Draw a picture of the two rows. Write how many children are in each row. **2.** The top row has four girls. The bottom row has four girls. Count how many girls and boys. Write the numbers.

Name ______________________

Lesson 7.7
Enrich

COMMON CORE STANDARD CC.K.NBT.1
Work with numbers 11–19 to gain foundations for place value.

Basketball Count

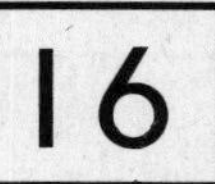

Red

Red **Blue**

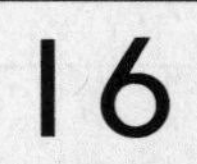

Red **Blue**

DIRECTIONS 1–2. The number shows how many basketballs in all. The Red team has 10 basketballs. Draw them. How many basketballs does the Blue team have? Draw them. 3. Draw different numbers of basketballs to show 16.

Name ______________________

COMMON CORE STANDARD CC.K.CC.3
Know number names and the count sequence.

How Many Oranges?

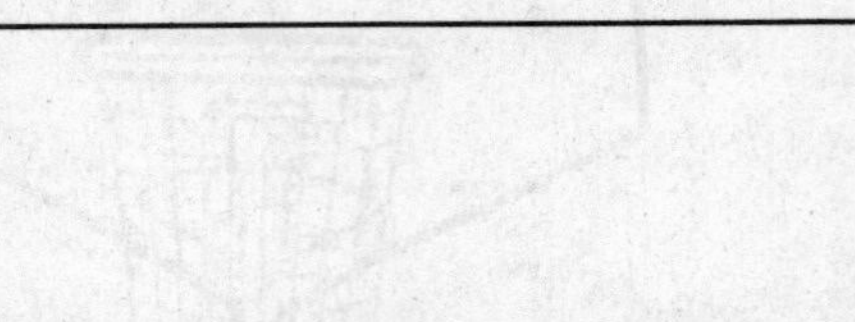

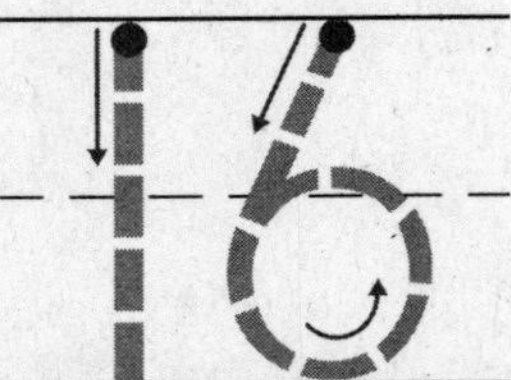

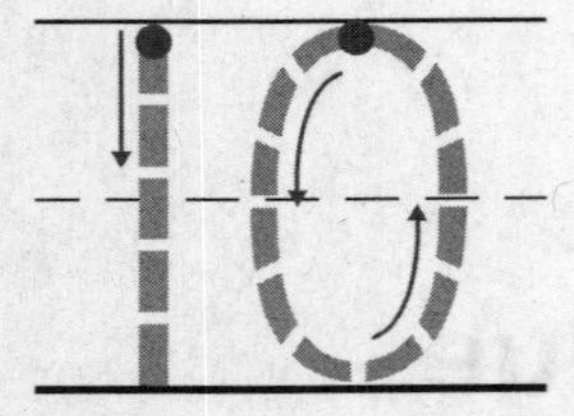

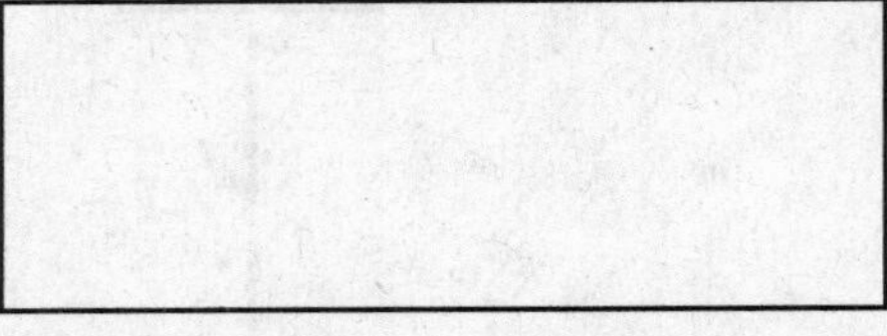

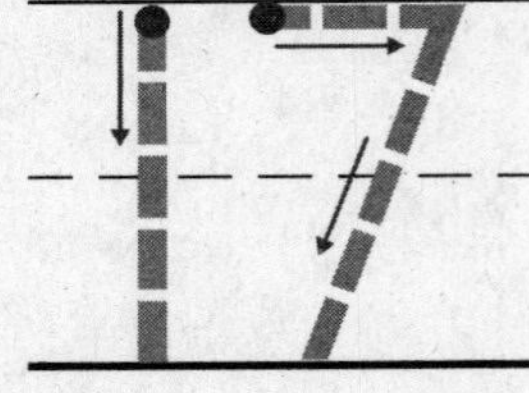

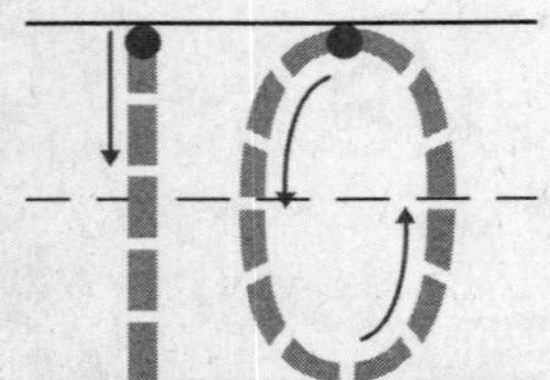

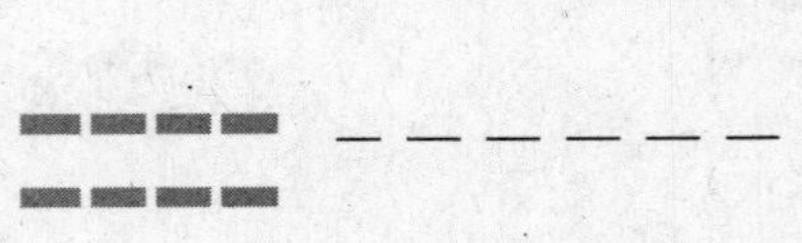

DIRECTIONS **1.** Draw 10 oranges on the first platter. Draw more oranges on the second platter to show 16. Trace the number. **2.** Look at the oranges you drew in Exercise 1. Complete the addition sentence to match. **3.** Draw 10 oranges on the first platter. Draw more oranges on the second platter to show 17. Trace the number. **4.** Look at the oranges you drew in Exercise 3. Complete the addition sentence to match.

Name ________________________

Fruit Baskets

COMMON CORE STANDARD CC.K.NBT.1
Work with numbers 11–19 to gain foundations for place value.

________ **apples and** ________ **apples**

________ **oranges and** ________ **oranges**

DIRECTIONS **1.** Draw 10 apples in the first basket. Draw more apples in the second basket to show 18. How many apples did you draw in each basket? Write the numbers. **2.** Draw 10 oranges in the first basket. Draw more oranges in the second basket to show 19. How many oranges did you draw in each basket? Write the numbers.

Name ____________________

COMMON CORE STANDARD CC.K.CC.3

Know number names and the count sequence.

Which One?

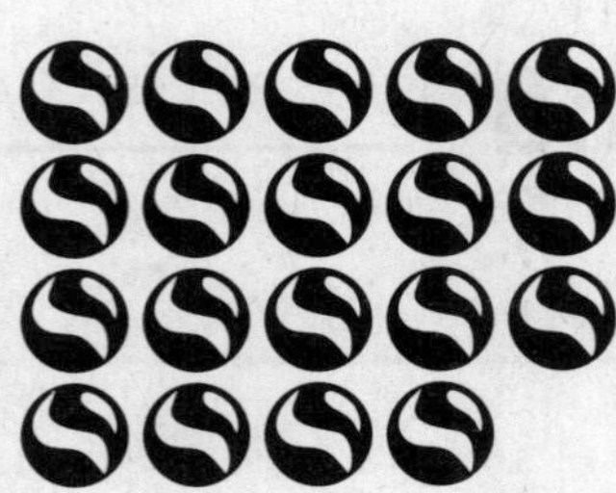

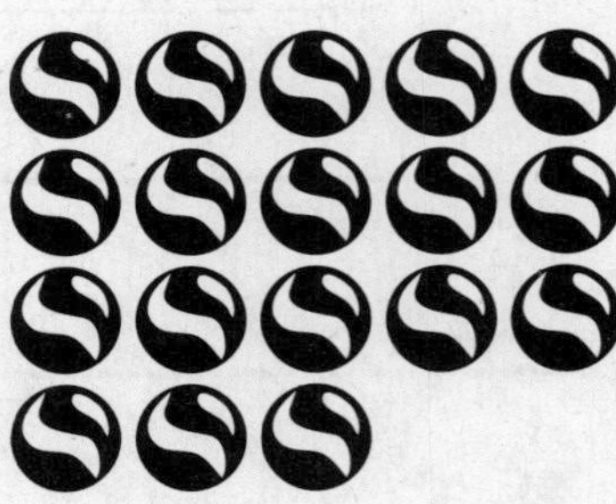

DIRECTIONS **1.** Kim has 10 stickers and nine stickers. Count the stickers. Write how many. Circle Kim's stickers. **2.** Ryan has 10 marbles and nine marbles. Count the marbles. Write how many. Circle Ryan's marbles. **3.** Sam draws 10 stars and eight stars. Count the stars. Write how many. Circle Sam's stars.

Name ___________________________

COMMON CORE STANDARD CC.K.CC.5
Count to tell the number of objects.

Count the Fireflies

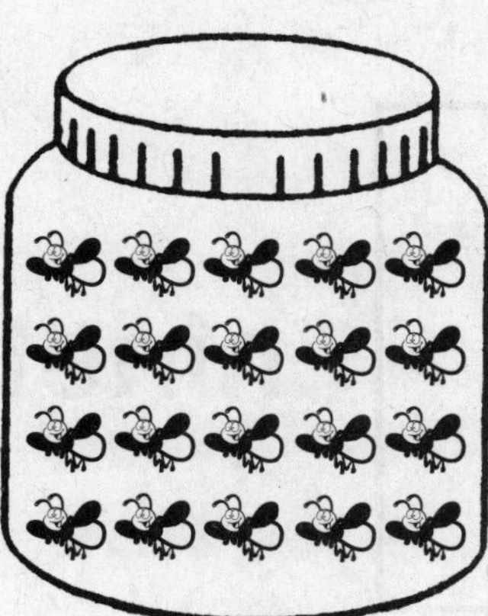

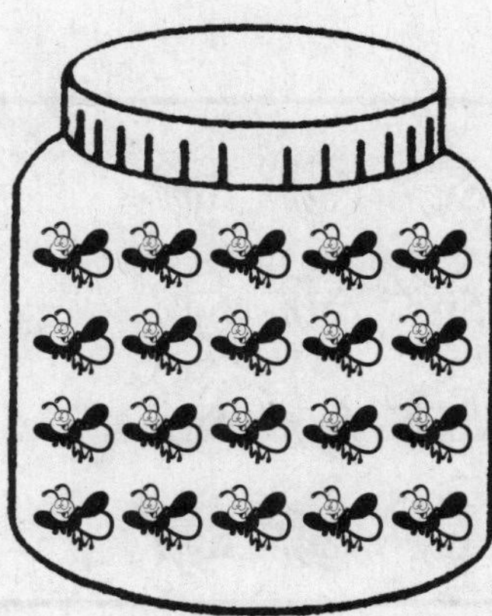

5

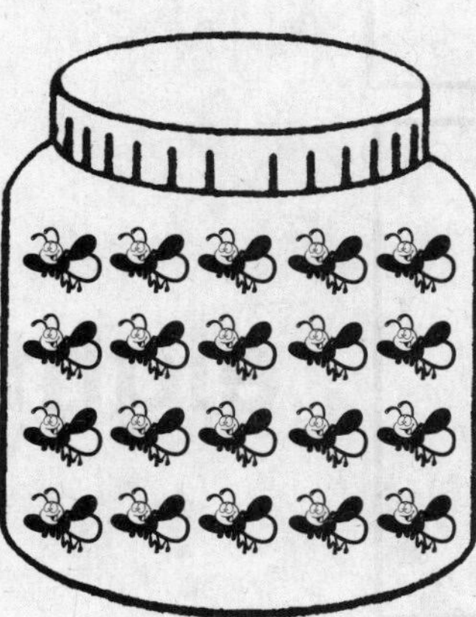

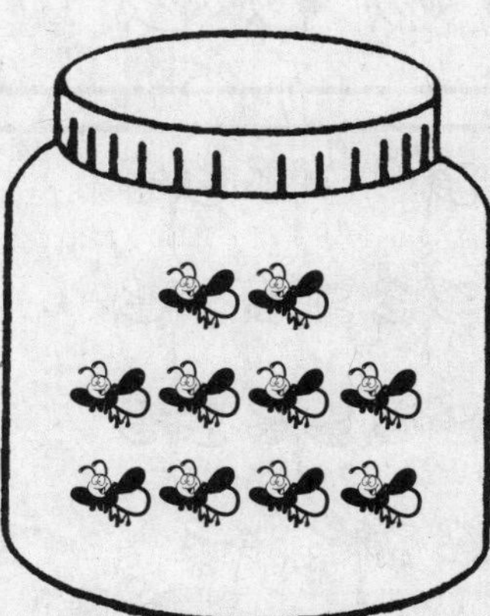

DIRECTIONS **1–6.** Count the fireflies in each jar. Circle the jars with 20 fireflies. Mark an X on the jars with less than 20 fireflies. Draw a line under any jars with more than 20 fireflies.

Name ______________________

COMMON CORE STANDARD CC.K.CC.3
Know number names and the count sequence.

Count and Match

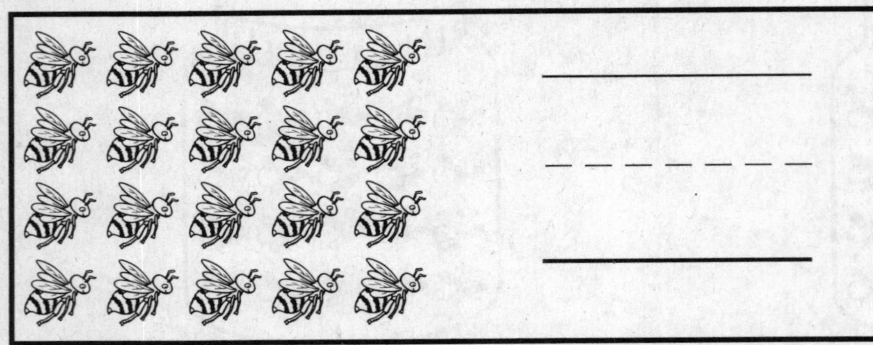

nineteen

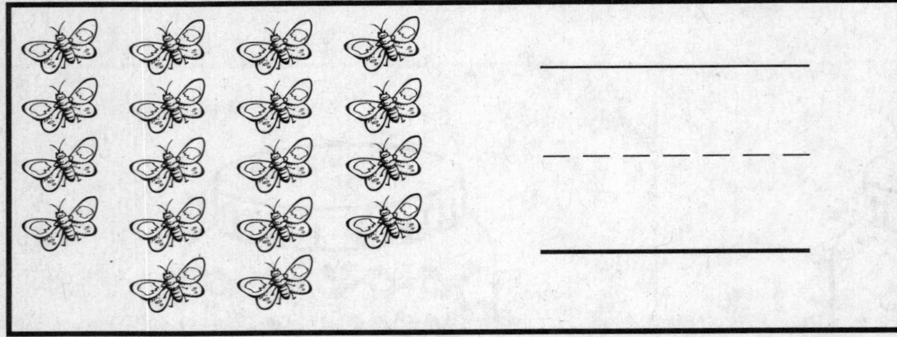

twenty

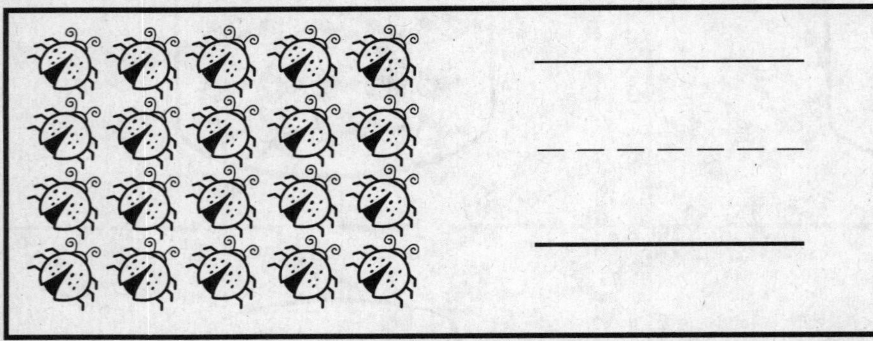

twenty

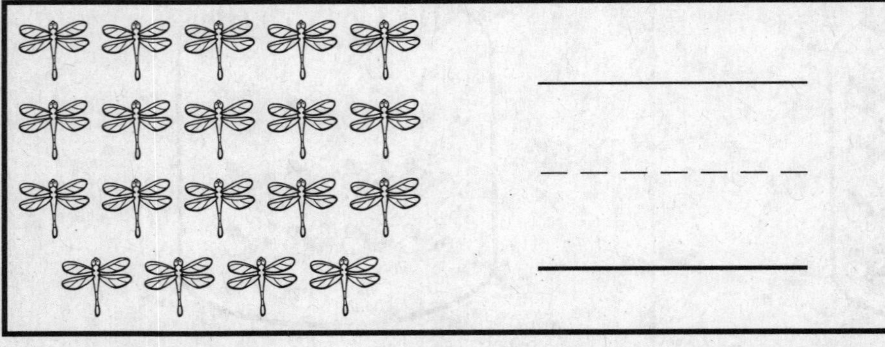

eighteen

DIRECTIONS 1. Count the insects in each group. Write the number. Draw a line to match the insects to the correct number word.

Name ______________________

Lesson 8.3
Enrich

COMMON CORE STANDARD CC.K.CC.2
Know number names and the count sequence.

Count Marbles

2

DIRECTIONS **1.** Count the marbles. Write the number of marbles in each set.
2. Write the numbers in order.

Name ______________________________

COMMON CORE STANDARD CC.K.CC.6
Compare numbers.

Compare Numbers

1

18

20

19

DIRECTIONS 1–3. Model the number with connecting cubes. Draw the cubes. Circle the set of 20 cubes. Draw a line under the set that has a number of cubes two less than 20. Mark an X on the set that has a number of cubes one less than 20.

Name ______________________________

Complete the Fifty Chart

COMMON CORE STANDARD CC.K.CC.1
Know number names and the count sequence.

1	2	3	4	5	6		8		10
11		13		15	16	17	18	19	20
21	22		24		26	27	28	29	30
31	32	33	34	35		37	38	39	40
41	42	43	44	45	46	47		49	50

DIRECTIONS 1. Point to each number as you count to 50. Tell the missing numbers. Find the number that is greater than 20 and less than 22. Circle the number. Find the number that is greater than 29 and less than 31. Draw a line under the number.

Name ____________________

COMMON CORE STANDARD CC.K.CC.1
Know number names and the count sequence.

Complete the Hundred Chart

1		3	4		6	7		9	10
11	12		14	15	16		18		20
	22	23	24		26		28	29	30
31	32	33		35	36	37		39	
41		43	44	45		47	48		50
51	52		54	55	56		58		60
	62	63	64		66	67		69	70
71	72			75	76	77	78	79	80
81	82	83	84				88	89	90
91					96	97	98	99	100

DIRECTIONS 1. Point to each number as you count to 100. Tell the missing numbers. Find the number that is greater than 76 and less than 78. Circle the number. Find the number that is greater than 98 and less than 100. Draw a line under the number.

Name ____________________

COMMON CORE STANDARD CC.K.CC.1
Know number names and the count sequence.

Color a Ten

1	2	3	4	5	6	7	8	9	10
11	12	13	14	15	16	17	18	19	20
21	22	23	24	25	26	27	28	29	30
31	32	33	34	35	36	37	38	39	40
41	42	43	44	45	46	47	48	49	50
51	52	53	54	55	56	57	58	59	60
61	62	63	64	65	66	67	68	69	70
71	72	73	74	75	76	77	78	79	80
81	82	83	84	85	86	87	88	89	90
91	92	93	94	95	96	97	98	99	100

DIRECTIONS 1. Count by tens as you point to the numbers. Then find the ten that is greater than 30 and less than 50. Color that number yellow. Find the ten that is greater than 80 and less than 100. Color that number orange. Find the ten that is greater than 60 and less than 80. Color that number red.

Name ______________________________

Color Sets of 10

COMMON CORE STANDARD CC.K.CC.1
Know number names and the count sequence.

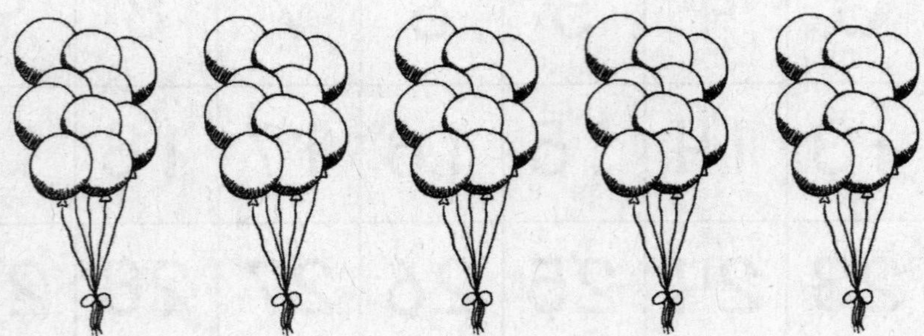

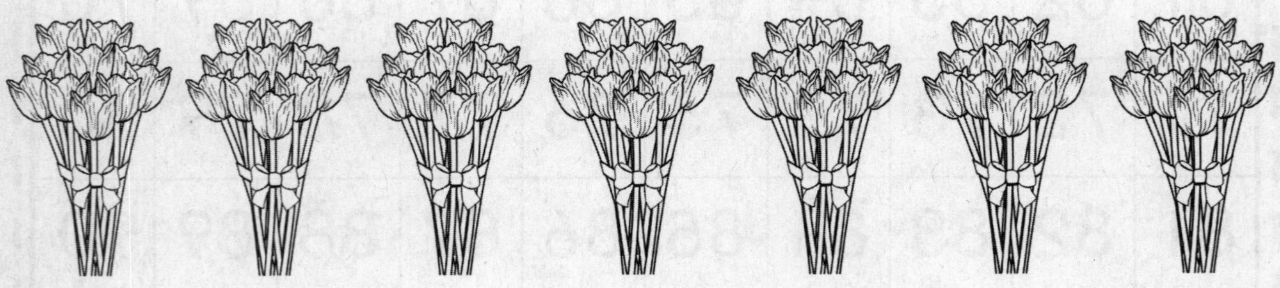

DIRECTIONS 1. Tori sees 20 green balloons and 30 orange balloons. The balloons are in sets of 10. All the balloons in each set are the same color. Color the balloons Tori sees. 2. John sees 10 yellow flowers, 20 purple flowers, and 40 red flowers. The flowers are in sets of 10. All the flowers in each set are the same color. Color the flowers John sees.

Name ____________________

Draw Sea Circles

COMMON CORE STANDARD CC.K.G.2
Identify and describe shapes (squares, circles, triangles, rectangles, hexagons, cubes, cones, cylinders, and spheres).

DIRECTIONS 1. Trace the fish and draw an underwater world using circles. Color your circles red. Then color the picture using other colors.

Name ______________________

COMMON CORE STANDARD CC.K.G.4
Analyze, compare, create, and compose shapes.

Complete the Circle

DIRECTIONS **1–3.** Finish each picture by completing the circle shape. Color the circle shapes.

Name ______________________

Do You See Squares?

COMMON CORE STANDARD CC.K.G.2
Identify and describe shapes (squares, circles, triangles, rectangles, hexagons, cubes, cones, cylinders, and spheres).

1

DIRECTIONS 1. Find and color the squares in the picture.

Name ______________________________

COMMON CORE STANDARD CC.K.G.4
Analyze, compare, create, and compose shapes.

Etch a Square

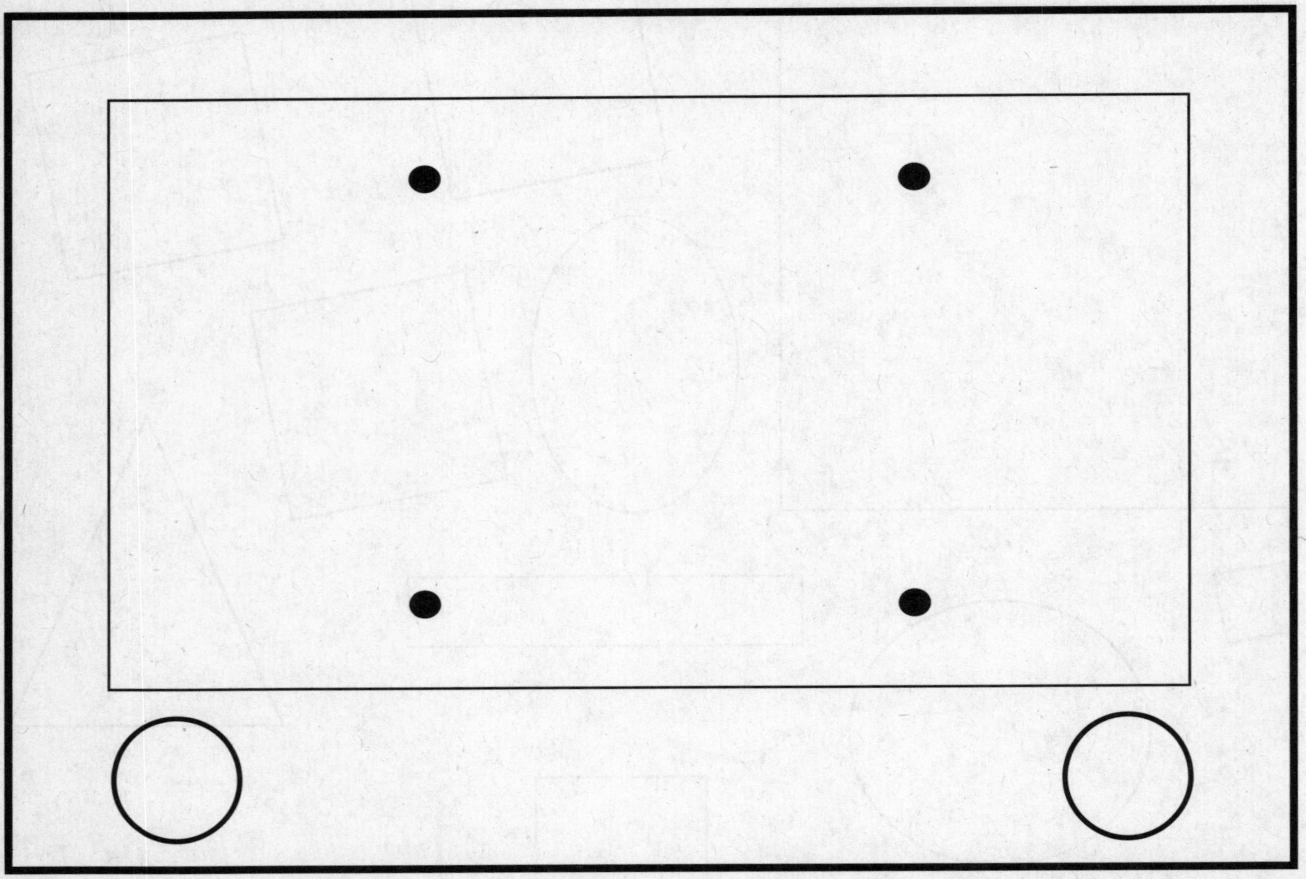

square

DIRECTIONS **1.** Place your pencil on the dot in the top right corner. Draw a line straight down to the dot in the bottom right corner. Then draw a line across the bottom to the dot in the bottom left corner. Draw a line straight up to the dot in the top left corner. Then draw a line across the top of the page to the dot where you began. Color the shape. **2.** Trace the name of the shape you drew.

Name ___________________________

Hidden Triangles

COMMON CORE STANDARD CC.K.G.2

Identify and describe shapes (squares, circles, triangles, rectangles, hexagons, cubes, cones, cylinders, and spheres).

DIRECTIONS 1. There are twelve triangles hiding in the picture. Find and color all of the triangles.

Name ___________________________

Lesson 9.6
Enrich

Triangle Repair

COMMON CORE STANDARD CC.K.G.4
Analyze, compare, create, and compose shapes.

1

DIRECTIONS 1. Some triangles are not finished. Draw the lines to complete the triangles. Color all the triangles.

Name ______________________________

COMMON CORE STANDARD CC.K.G.2
Identify and describe shapes (squares, circles, triangles, rectangles, hexagons, cubes, cones, cylinders, and spheres).

Find the Rectangles

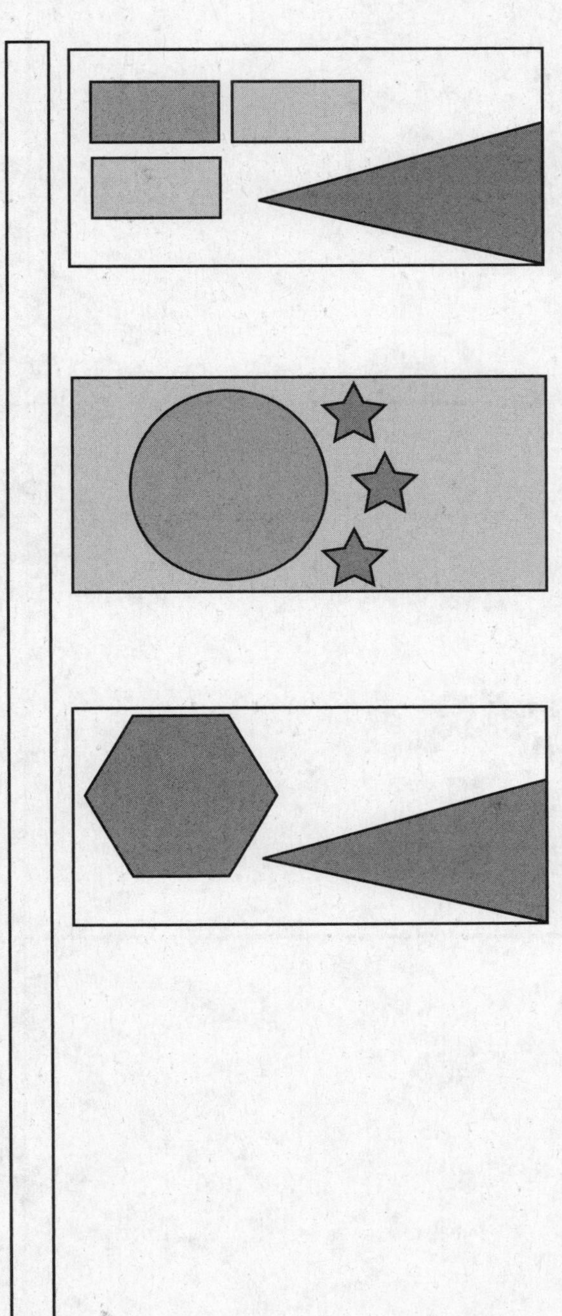

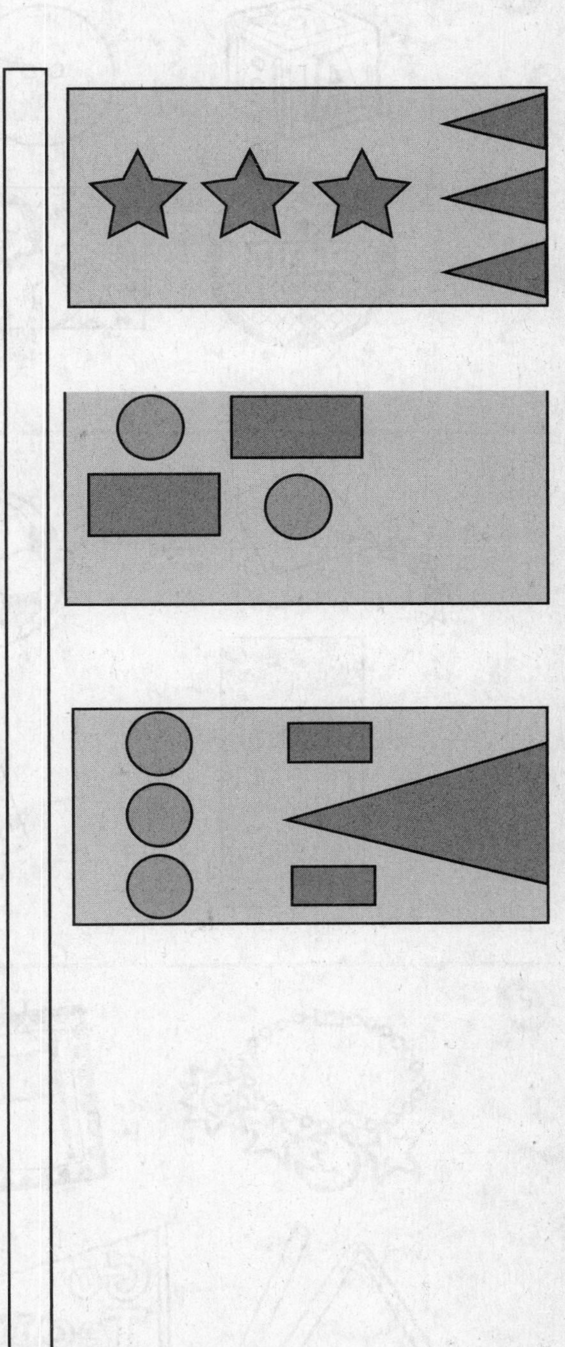

DIRECTIONS 1. Every flag on this page is shaped like a rectangle. Circle the flags that have smaller rectangles on them. Then circle the smaller rectangles in the flags. Mark an X on the flags that do not have smaller rectangles on them.

Name ______________________

COMMON CORE STANDARD CC.K.G.4
Analyze, compare, create, and compose shapes.

Match That Shape

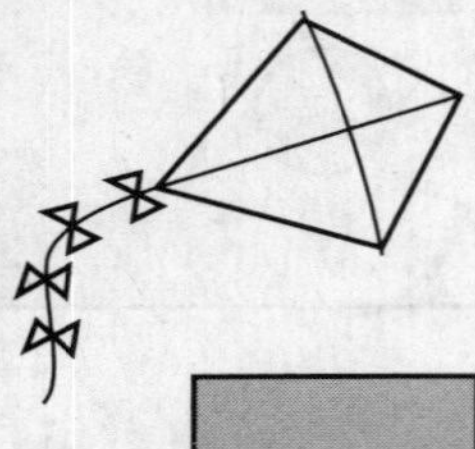

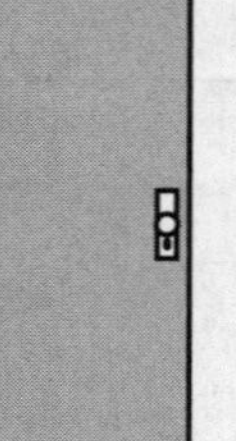

DIRECTIONS 1–3. Circle the object that is a rectangle. Draw the object.

Name ________________________________

Hexagon Design

COMMON CORE STANDARD CC.K.G.2
Identify and describe shapes (squares, circles, triangles, rectangles, hexagons, cubes, cones, cylinders, and spheres).

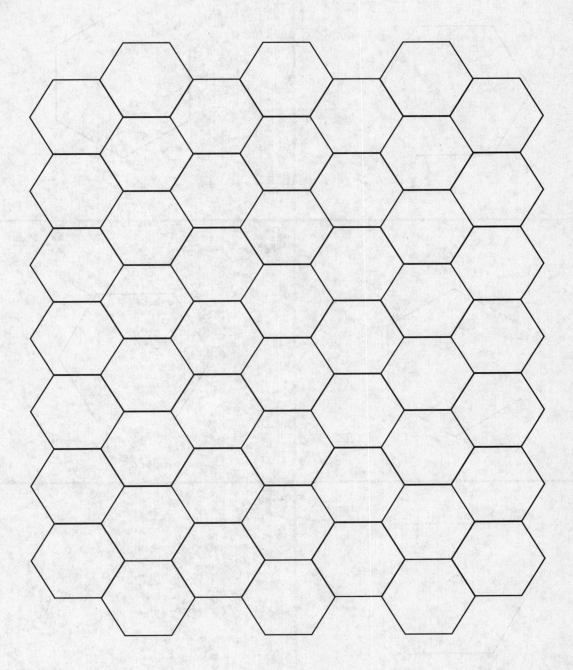

DIRECTIONS 1. Color the hexagons to make a picture or design. Use different colors.

Name ________________________________

Happy Hexagons

COMMON CORE STANDARD CC.K.G.4
Analyze, compare, create, and compose shapes.

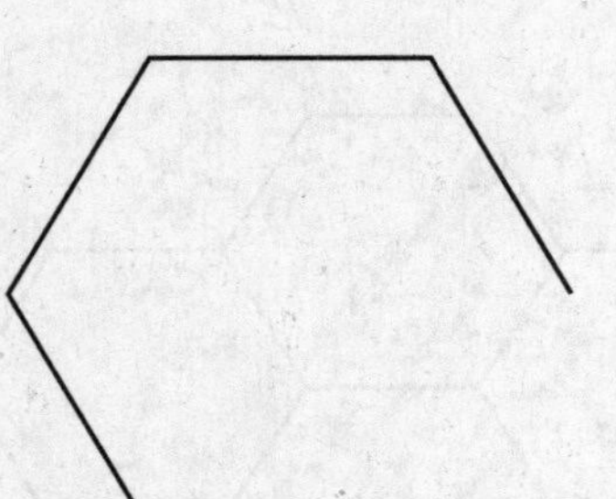

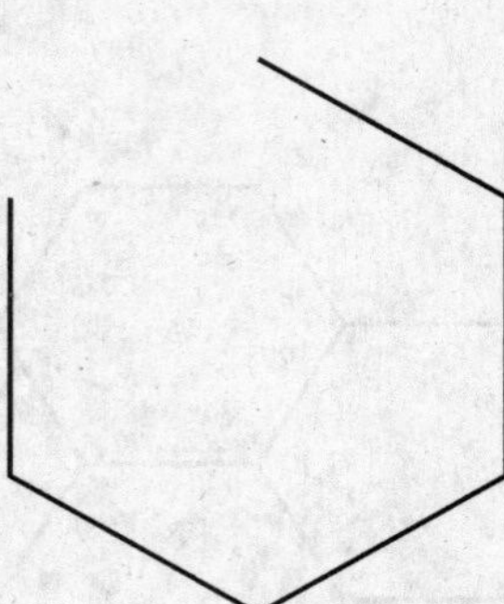

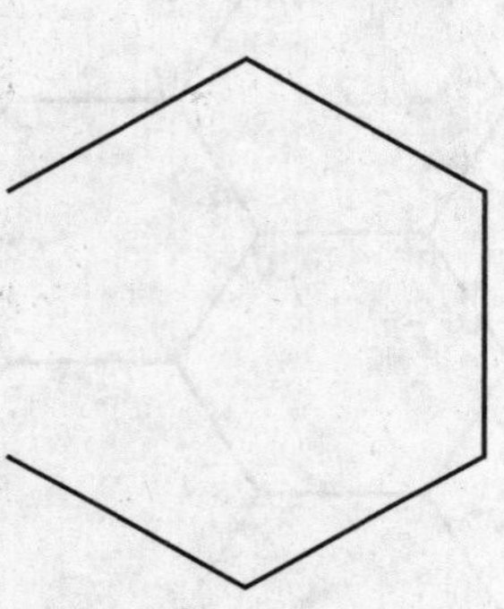

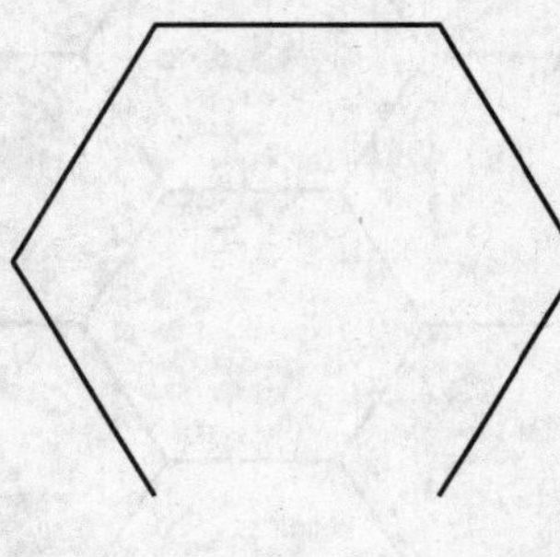

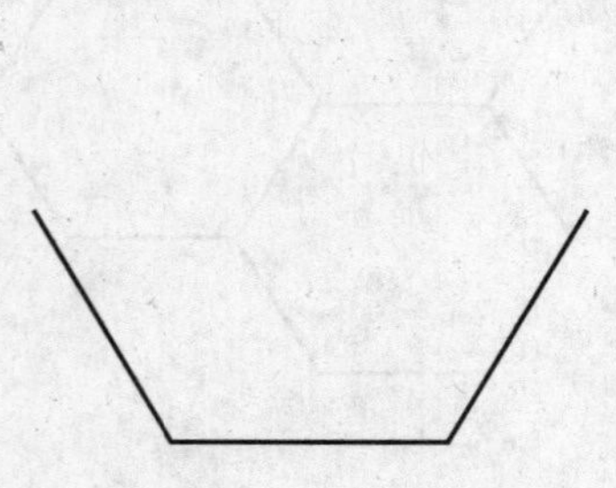

DIRECTIONS **1–5.** Draw to complete the hexagon. Color the hexagon.
6. Draw a hexagon. Color your hexagon.

Name ______________________________

Sort Spilled Shapes

COMMON CORE STANDARD CC.K.G.4
Analyze, compare, create, and compose shapes.

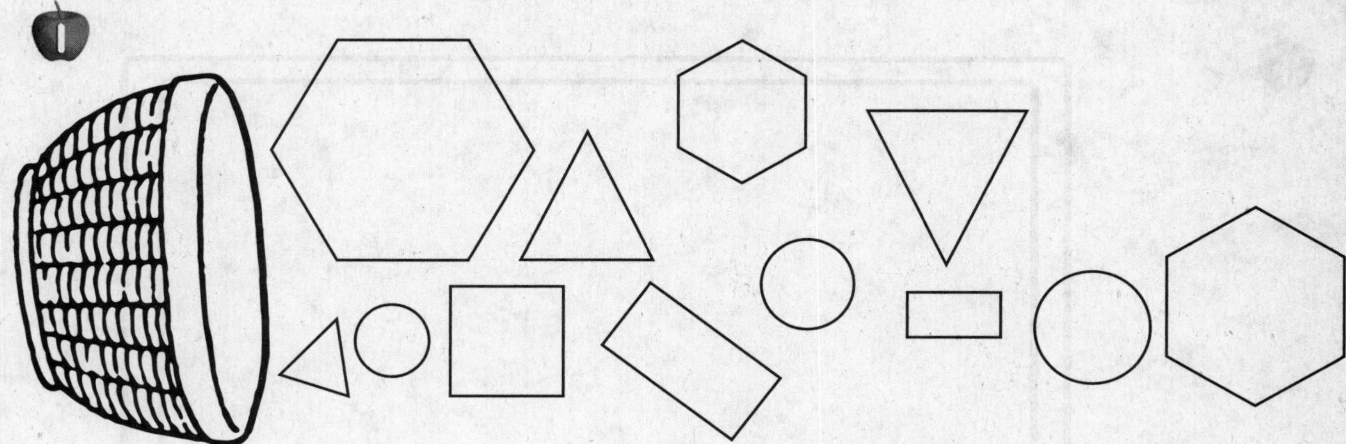

curved	3 sides
4 sides	**6 vertices**

DIRECTIONS 1. Sort the shapes that have spilled out of the basket. Draw and color the shapes in the correct sorting box.

Name ______________________

COMMON CORE STANDARD CC.K.G.6
Analyze, compare, create, and compose shapes.

Draw a Shape

DIRECTIONS **1.** Draw a shape with three sides and three corners, or vertices. **2.** Join some shapes like the one you drew in Exercise 1 to make another shape. How many new shapes can you make? Draw them.

Name ________________________________

COMMON CORE STANDARD CC.K.G.4
Analyze, compare, create, and compose shapes.

Three-Dimensional Cleanup

DIRECTIONS 1. Use blue to color the objects that roll but do not stack. Use green to color the objects that stack but do not roll. Use red to color the objects that roll and stack. Circle the objects that slide.

Name ______________________________

Shopping for Spheres

COMMON CORE STANDARD CC.K.G.2
Identify and describe shapes (squares, circles, triangles, rectangles, hexagons, cubes, cones, cylinders, and spheres).

DIRECTIONS 1. Circle the objects that are shaped like a sphere. Color those objects.

Name ____________________

Race to Find the Cubes

COMMON CORE STANDARD CC.K.G.2
Identify and describe shapes (squares, circles, triangles, rectangles, hexagons, cubes, cones, cylinders, and spheres).

DIRECTIONS 1. Find the objects that are shaped like a cube. Color those objects.

Name ___________________________

Dot to Dot Cylinders

COMMON CORE STANDARD CC.K.G.2
Identify and describe shapes (squares, circles, triangles, rectangles, hexagons, cubes, cones, cylinders, and spheres).

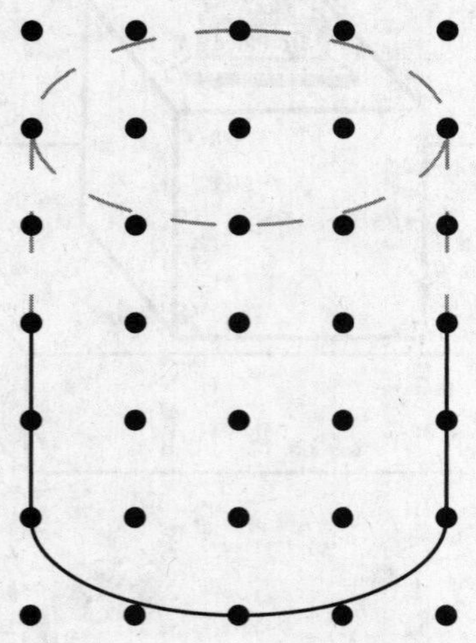

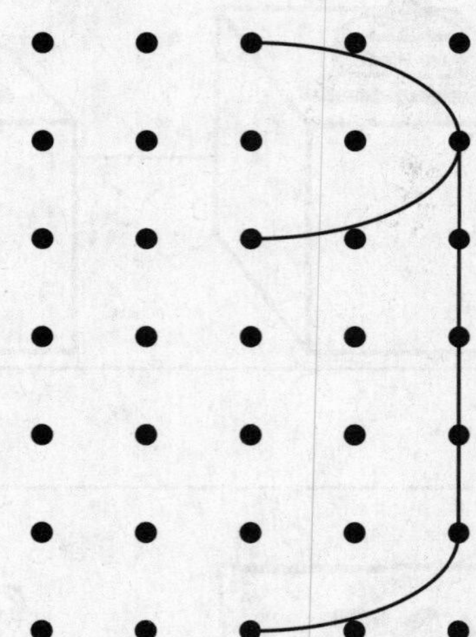

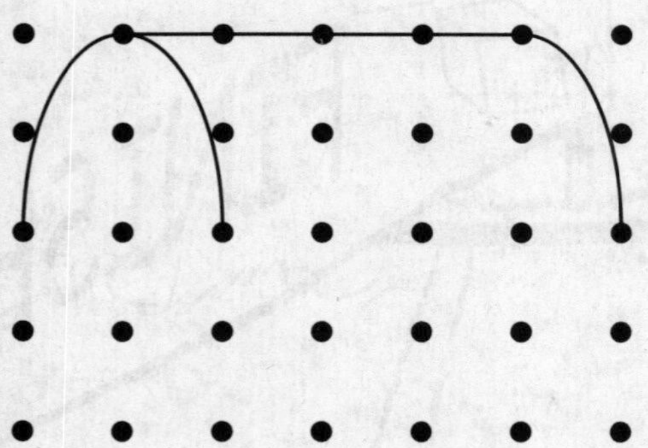

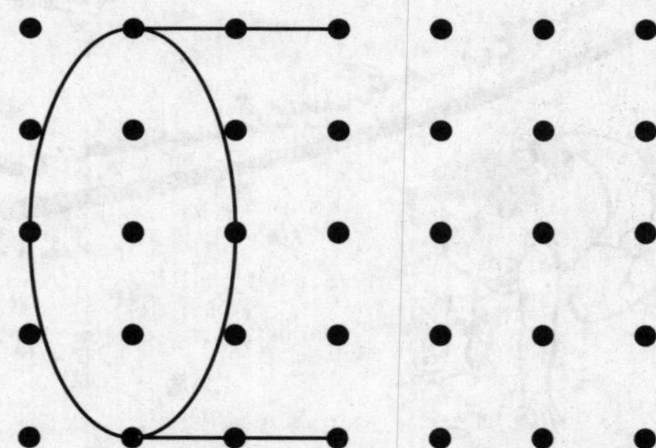

DIRECTIONS I. Trace or draw to complete each cylinder.

Name ______________________________

COMMON CORE STANDARD CC.K.G.2
Identify and describe shapes (squares, circles, triangles, rectangles, hexagons, cubes, cones, cylinders, and spheres).

Where Are the Cones?

DIRECTIONS 1. Draw a circle around the objects that are shaped like a cone. Color those objects.

Name ______________________________

Trace and Draw

COMMON CORE STANDARD CC.K.G.3
Identify and describe shapes (squares, circles, triangles, rectangles, hexagons, cubes, cones, cylinders, and spheres).

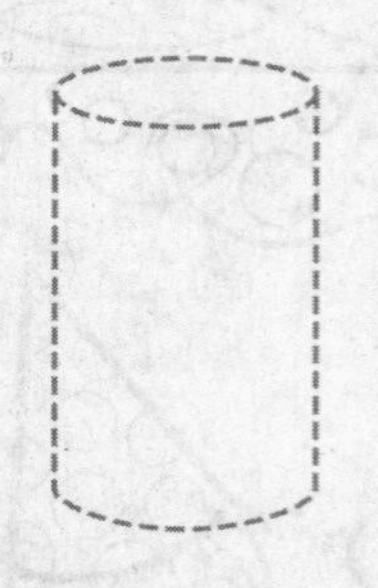

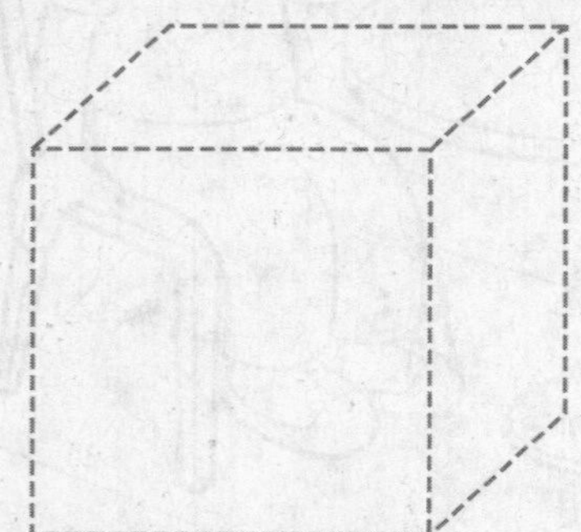

DIRECTIONS 1–3. Trace the shape. Then draw the shape. Use yellow to color any flat shapes. Use green to color any solid shapes.

Name ____________________

COMMON CORE STANDARD CC.K.G.1
Identify and describe shapes (squares, circles, triangles, rectangles, hexagons, cubes, cones, cylinders, and spheres).

Above and Below Shapes

1

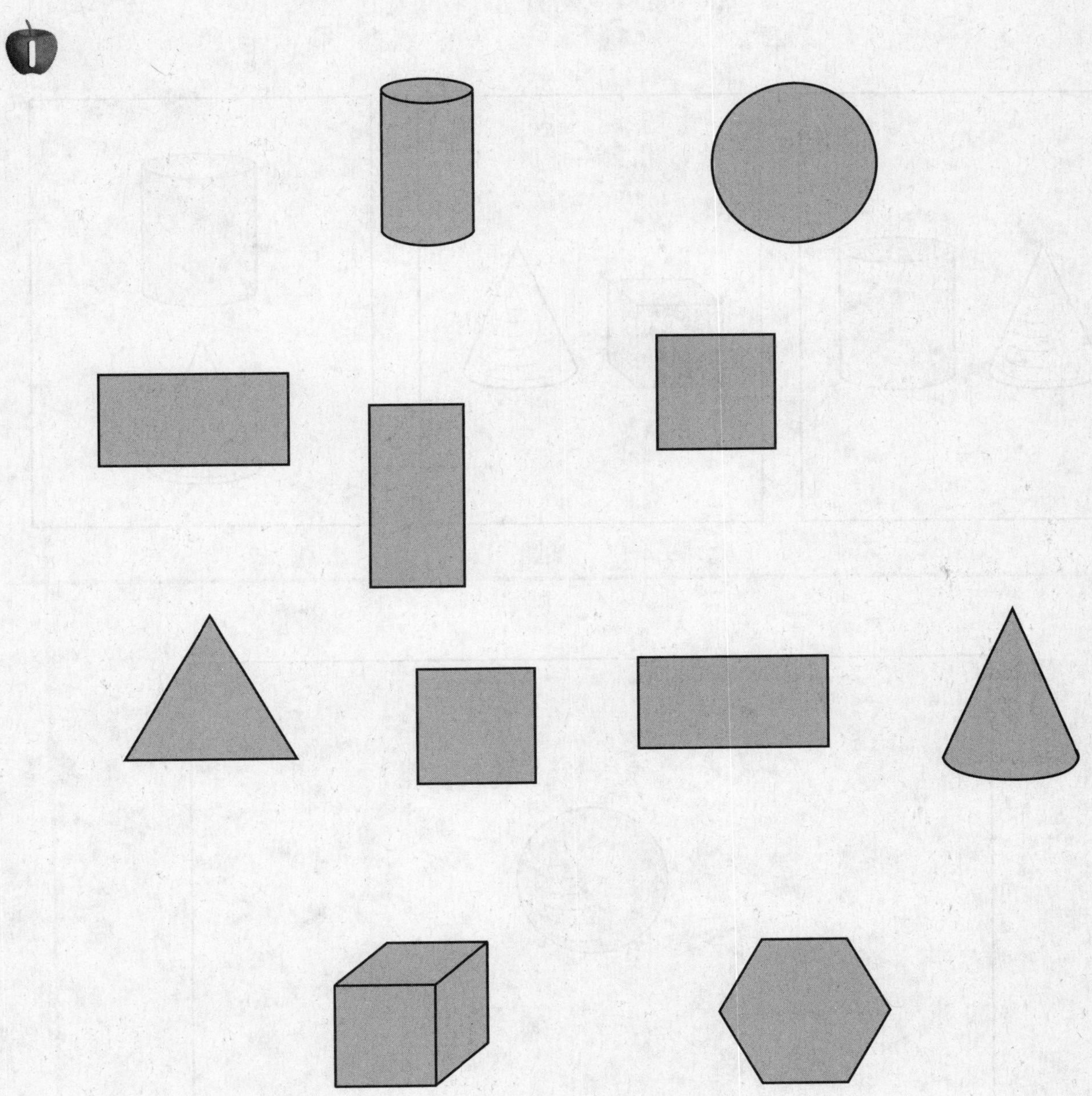

DIRECTIONS **1.** Draw a dot below the cylinder. Draw a dot below the circle. Draw a dot above the cone. Draw a dot above the hexagon. Draw a dot above the cube. Draw a dot above the triangle. Connect the dots to draw a hexagon.

Name ______________________________

Where Is the Cone?

COMMON CORE STANDARD CC.K.G.1
Identify and describe shapes (squares, circles, triangles, rectangles, hexagons, cubes, cones, cylinders, and spheres).

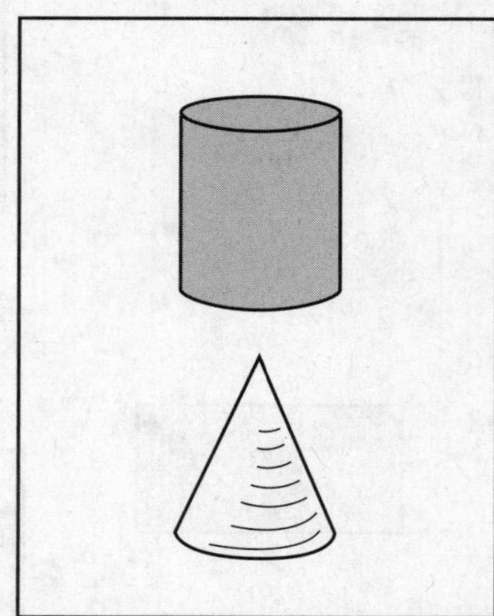

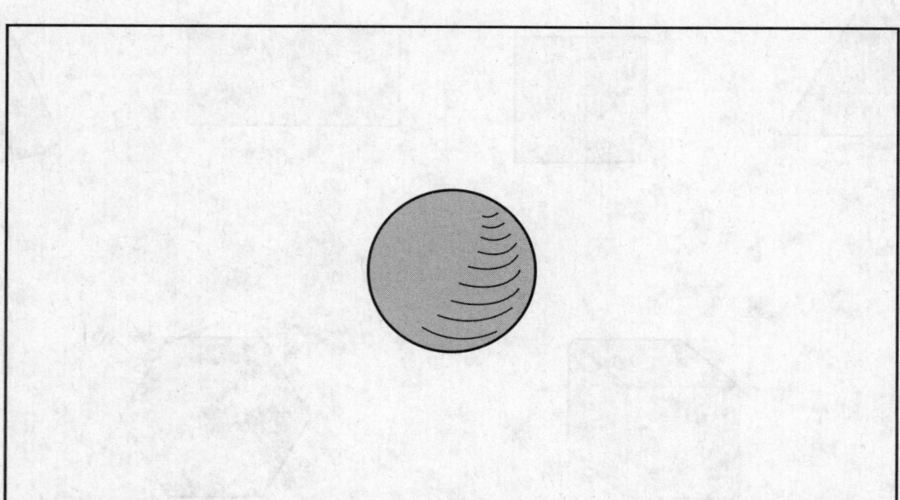

DIRECTIONS **1.** Find the cone that is below the cylinder. Color that cone red. Find the cone that is beside the cylinder. Color that cone blue. Find the cone that is next to the cube. Color that cone yellow. **2.** Draw a cone near the sphere. Use the words *above, below, next to,* or *beside* to name the position of that cone.

Name ____________________

COMMON CORE STANDARD CC.K.G.1
Identify and describe shapes (squares, circles, triangles, rectangles, hexagons, cubes, cones, cylinders, and spheres).

Shapes and Shelves

DIRECTIONS 1. Find the object on the floor that is shaped like a cylinder. Draw it on the shelf beside the object that is shaped like a cone. Find the object on the floor that is shaped like a cone. Draw it on the shelf below the object that is shaped like a sphere. Find the object on the floor that is shaped like a sphere. Draw it on the shelf in front of the object that is shaped like a cube. Find the object on the floor that is shaped like a cube. Draw it anywhere on the shelves. Where did you draw it?

Name ______________________________

Lesson II.I
Enrich

Ribbon Lengths

COMMON CORE STANDARD CC.K.MD.2

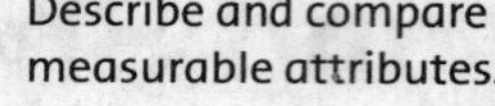

Describe and compare measurable attributes.

1

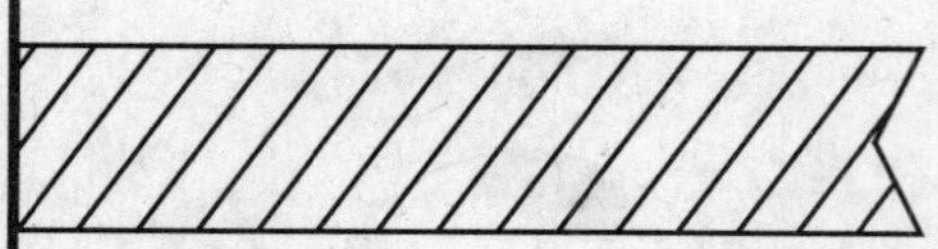

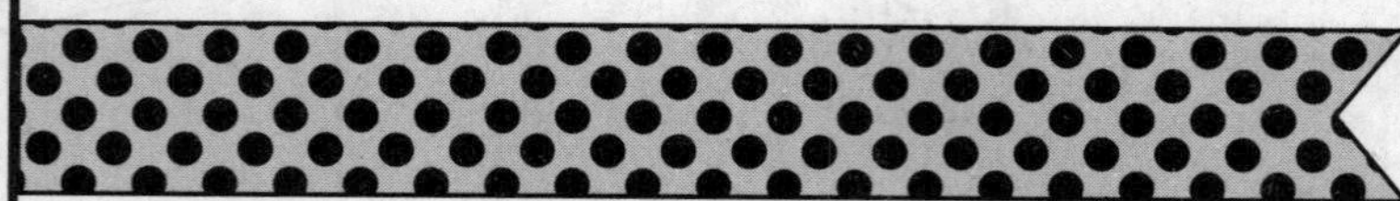

DIRECTIONS **1.** Draw a ribbon that is longer than the ribbon shown. Color your ribbon. **2.** Draw a ribbon that is shorter than the ribbon shown. Color your ribbon. **3.** Draw a ribbon that is about the same length as the ribbon shown. Color your ribbon.

Name ______________________________________

Shorter and Taller Sunflowers

COMMON CORE STANDARD CC.K.MD.2
Describe and compare measurable attributes.

DIRECTIONS 1. Draw a sunflower that is shorter than the one shown.
2. Draw a sunflower that is taller than the one shown.

Name ______________________________

COMMON CORE STANDARD CC.K.MD.2
Describe and compare measurable attributes.

Compare and Draw

DIRECTIONS 1. Find a small classroom object. Place one end of the object on the line. Draw the object. Compare the length of your drawing to other objects in the classroom. Find an object that is shorter than the length of your drawing. Draw that object. Circle the shorter drawing. 2. Find a small classroom object. Place one end of the object on the line. Draw the object. Compare the height of your drawing to other objects in the classroom. Find an object that is shorter than the height of your drawing. Draw that object. Circle the shorter drawing.

Name ______________________________

Kitchen Weights

COMMON CORE STANDARD CC.K.MD.2
Describe and compare measurable attributes.

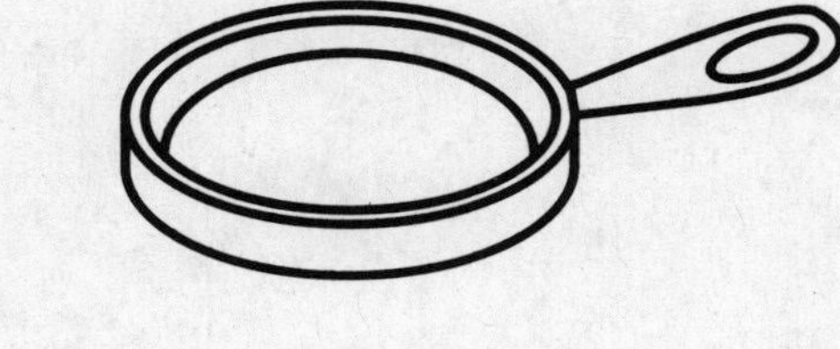

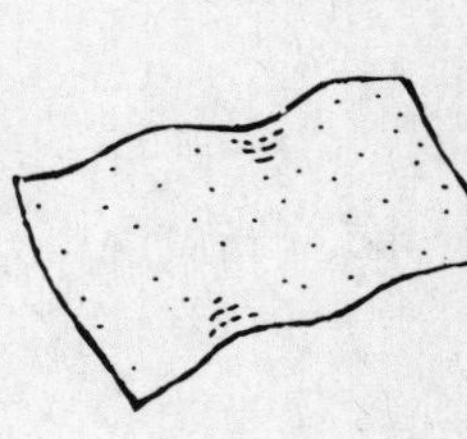

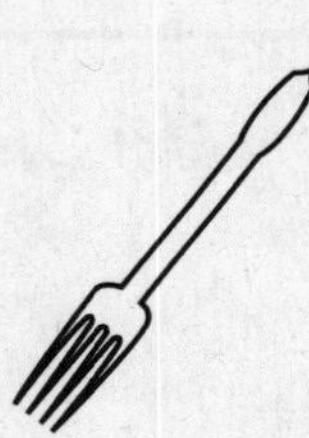

DIRECTIONS **1.** Circle the objects that are lighter than the object in the top row. Mark an X on the objects that are heavier. **2.** Circle the objects that are heavier than the object in the top row. Mark an X on the objects that are lighter.

Name ________________________________

COMMON CORE STANDARD K.MD.1
Describe and compare measurable attributes.

Ways to Measure Toys

DIRECTIONS Use red to trace the line that shows how to measure the length of each object. Use blue to trace the line that shows how to measure the height of each object. **1.** Draw a toy train that is longer than the one shown. Tell about the lengths of the trains. Talk about another way to measure the trains. **2.** Draw a toy bear that is taller than the one shown. Make your bear taller than the one shown. Tell about the heights of the bears. Talk about another way to measure the bears.

Name ______________________________

COMMON CORE STANDARD CC.K.MD.3
Classify objects and count the number of objects in each category.

Which Does Not Belong?

1

2

3

DIRECTIONS **1–3.** Look at the shapes. Tell what is the same about most of the shapes. Find the shape that does not belong. Mark an X on it.

Name ____________________

Sort Shapes

COMMON CORE STANDARD CC.K.MD.3
Classify objects and count the number of objects in each category.

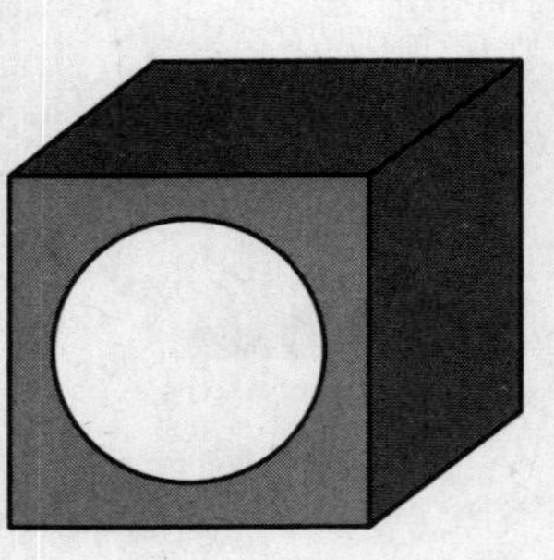

 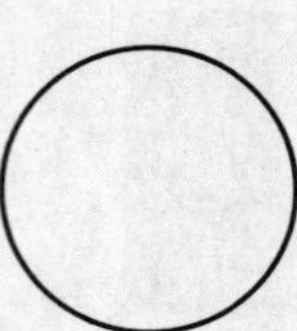  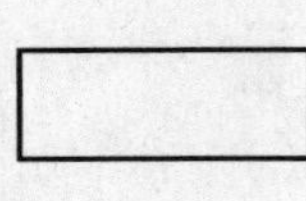

 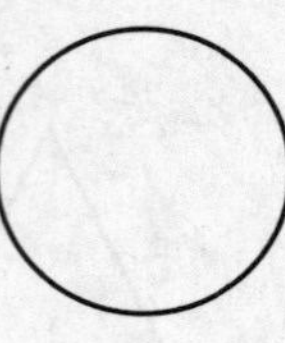 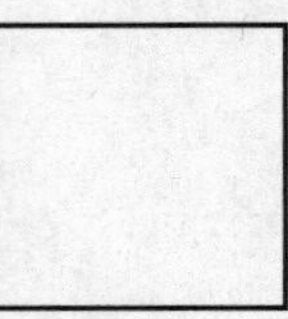 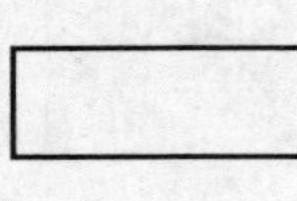

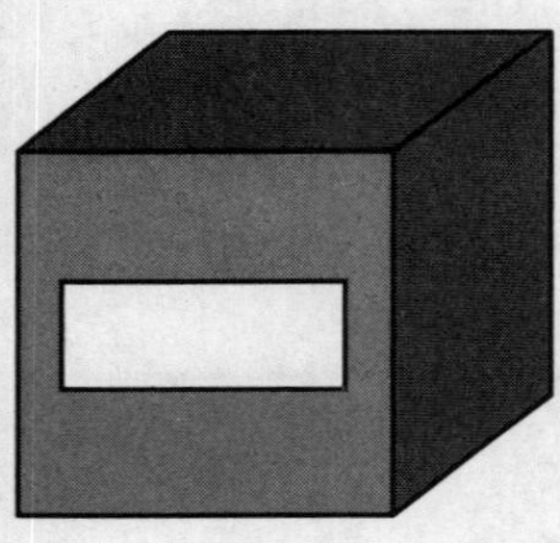

  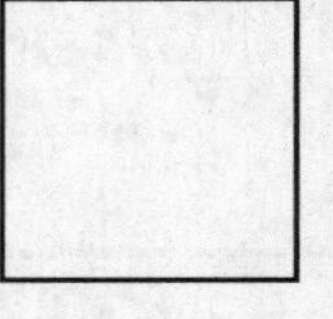 

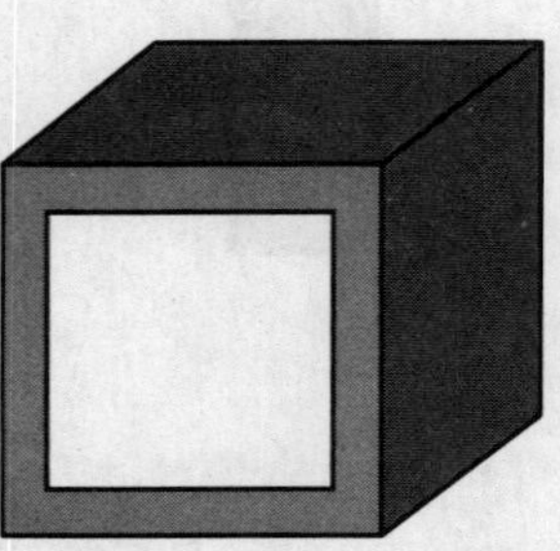

  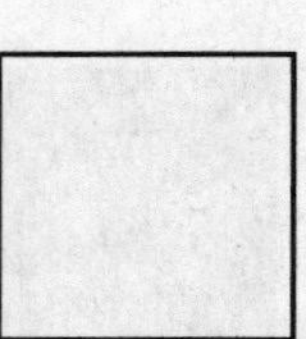 

DIRECTIONS **1–4.** Look at the shape on the shape sorter box. Mark an X on the shape that matches the shape on the shape sorter box.

Name ______________________________

COMMON CORE STANDARD CC.K.MD.3
Classify objects and count the number of objects in each category.

Size and Shape

1

2

3 **big** **small**

DIRECTIONS 1. Circle the big shape. 2. Circle the small shape. 3. Draw a set of big shapes and a set of small shapes on the sorting mat.

Name ____________________

Make Your Own Graph

COMMON CORE STANDARD CC.K.MD.3
Classify objects and count the number of objects in each category.

1

Red, Blue, and Green Cubes					
R					
B					
G					

2

R ______

B ______

G ______

DIRECTIONS **1.** Make a graph using red, blue, and green cubes. R is for red, B is for blue, and G is for green. Use a different number of cubes for each color. Draw and color the cubes. **2.** Write how many of each color.

Name ____________________

Crates of Fruit

COMMON CORE STANDARD CC.K.MD.3
Classify objects and count the number of objects in each category.

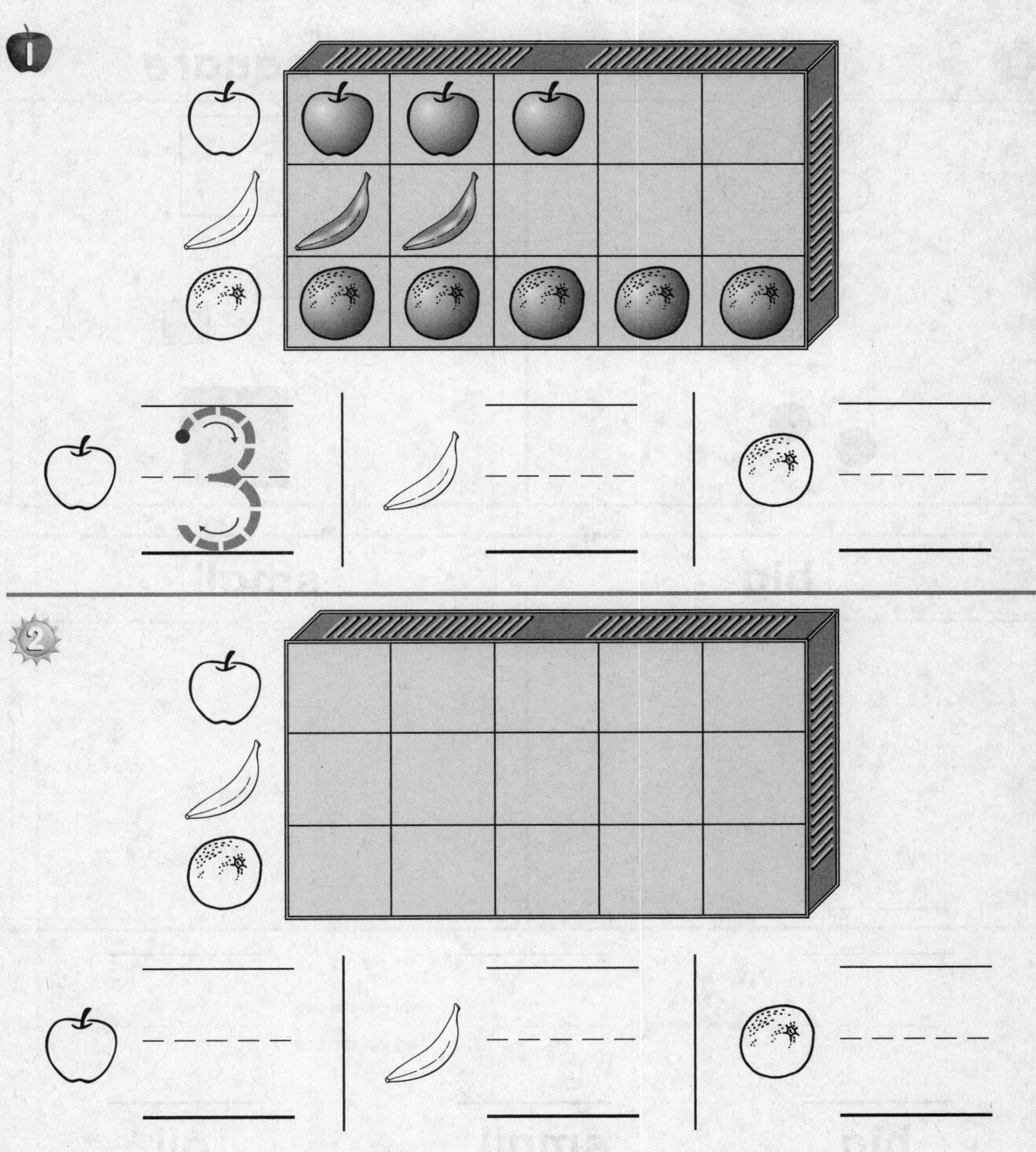

DIRECTIONS **1.** Count how many of each type of fruit is in the crate. Color the fruit and write the number. **2.** Draw your own fruit in the crate. Count how many of each type of fruit is in the crate. Color the fruit and write the number.

Name ____________________

Sorting Three Ways

COMMON CORE STANDARD CC.K.MD.3
Classify objects and count the number of objects in each category.

1 **circle** **square**

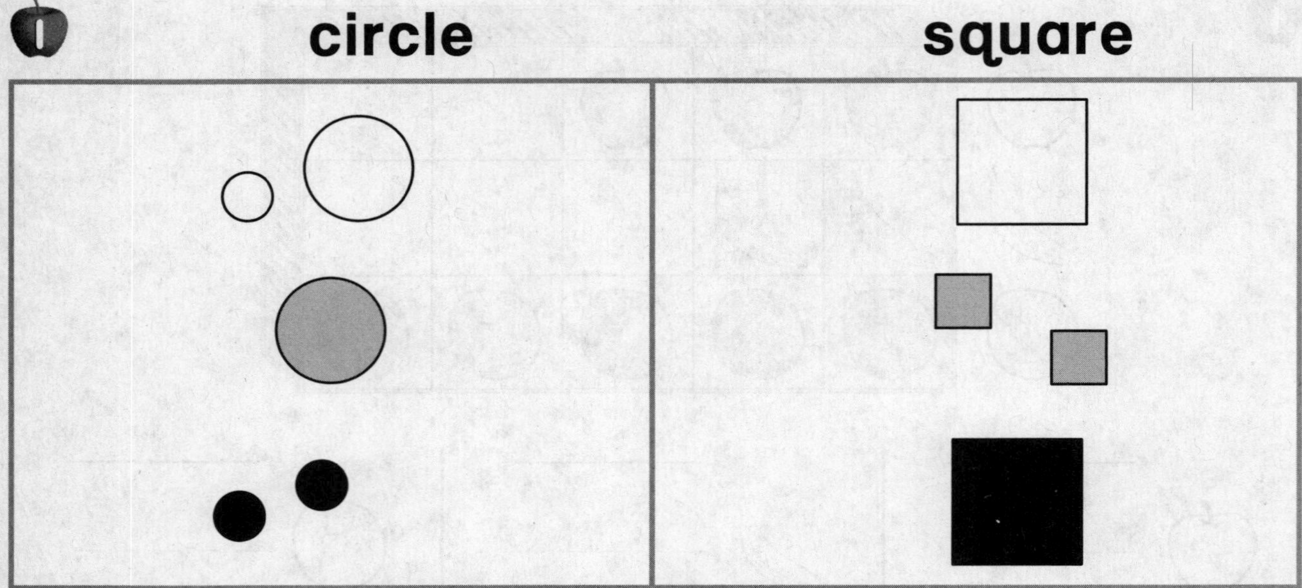

2 **big** **small**

____ + ____ = ____

big **small** **all**

DIRECTIONS 1. Look at the sorting mat. How are the shapes sorted? Draw lines on the sorting mat to show how the shapes can also be sorted by color. 2. Show another way the shapes can be sorted. Draw the shapes on the sorting mat. How many big and small shapes did you draw? Write and trace to complete the addition sentence.